The
Folksinger's
Daughter

The Folksinger's Daughter

Jeannie Brand

2017

New Street Communications, LLC

Wickford, RI

Published May 2017 by
New Street Communications, LLC
Wickford, Rhode Island
newstreetcommunications.com

Dedicated To My Father

OSCAR BRAND

Who Always Encouraged Me To Write
And Was My Hero

*Oscar Brand shown with (from left): Songwriters Betty Comden
and Adolph Green, Eleanor Roosevelt, and singer Lola Fisher backstage at
Carnegie Hall, 1962.*
(Associated Press Photo.)

Prologue

This is the first sentence of something, but I do not know what or where it will lead. Maybe nowhere, maybe just a diary. Maybe someone, sometime will like it and find it interesting or helpful or just entertaining. I doubt the entertaining part. What I have to say isn't always kind or easy, but it's truthful. I like the truth. Lies, well, I believe you always get caught.

Admittedly, I'm scared. I think I might hurt someone's feelings along the way. Or, someone might read this and decide I shouldn't have written it down. But I think I should.

Once the decision is made to write, every thought comes racing in screaming: *Me! Me! Pick me! For story. I'm the most interesting!* But the truth is, stream of consciousness would be an asset here, since every thought is jumbled like a smoothie in a blender. It's all an irregular heartbeat of a life. Mother and father make baby and siblings. Then have some weird situations. It makes for a good sitcom. But my life was not a sitcom; it was a mixed-up paradox of what childhood should be.

I am not alone, granted. Many children of the 50's had similar experiences. The Boomers wanted so much to have their parents' idea of success, but on closer examination, even the parents really never had it either. So this is my story. As best as I can recall. With no need to exaggerate, I assure you.

Chapter One

My parents were famous. Actually, my father was more famous after I was born than before; and my mother stopped being famous the second she married my father, except for the brief time she tried to paint.

My father suffered from polio when he was a child growing up in Winnipeg, Manitoba. He used to tell us there were two seasons there: *The Winter* and *The Thaw*. One day, laying in bed, believing he had not much of a future at all, the idea occurred that he might become a writer. After all, this would be one of the only things he could do from bed or in an iron lung at worst. But this was not to be.

When he was still young, Dad's parents moved to Brooklyn, New York, where an experimental polio treatment was available. They left behind considerable property and family, solely to save my father's life. Three children were treated, two died; my father survived. He was able to walk upright, unaided, for the rest of his life, one leg two inches shorter than the other, disguised with orthotics he fashioned out of cardboard and rubber cement.

Dad used to joke that his family arrived "just in time for the Great Depression." This seemed funny to us, all the crazy jobs and survival techniques families used back then. At one point, Dad even took a job changing the letters by hand on the board at the New York Stock Exchange.

I guess it's a good time to mention that we're Jewish – although we've left most of the dogma behind. That's the way the family wanted to live.

Dad was enrolled in Brooklyn College at the start of World War II. He waited tables for expenses and food, and performed in every school play available. His brother had left to join the Army, and as soon as he graduated, Dad tried to enlist. But he was 4F.

Polio kept him out; plus his eyesight was terrible. Still, his desire to serve was so great that he memorized the eye chart and eventually found the one doctor who agreed to sign off on the polio so long as Dad agreed to remain stateside. Thus, even though he won a sharp shooter medal in Basic Training, Dad wound up working in a psychiatric hospital, helping what was then known as the returning "shell shocked" veterans. These days we know it as Post Traumatic Stress Disorder (PTSD).

All this history is important because my father's career came about on account of this assignment. Being a natural entertainer, he found that communication with his patients was possible with song. It built trust and was a huge part of the trauma recovery program. Many veterans taught him songs they had learned in the armed forces. Later, my father would record them and they would help build his career and following. These include bawdy songs which at the time felt quite risqué, but now seem tame. He earned the moniker, *The Bawdy Balladeer*, which I assure you was no fun for me, as it seemed to stick no matter what other accomplishments he went on to have.

Dad went on tour after the war with a few successful albums behind him and a little place on West 12th Street in "the Village." Yup, *that* Village. Greenwich Village. The famous neighborhood of artists of all types, bohemians, and constant challenging of the "establishment." The Village of *change*. A community of musicians, painters, writers: people who loved and supported each other.

By the time he was 26, my father had established a successful radio show on WNYC, born after an offer to do a free Christmas program and morphing into the weekly *Folksong Festival* program, today having run for more than 70 years and counting: thus an item in the *Guinness Book of World Records*.

This program – running every Sunday night at 6pm – enjoyed great popularity, because it not only showcased known talent and traditional music, but my father also included new and emerging talent who were invited to stop by and sit in live, and talk and play.

A new wave of folk music had taken hold. Not just traditional songs, but also new, unique, and discomforting ballads of social protest. Dad showcased it all.

Fortunately, we have the archive tapes, which hold such gems as Bob Dylan's first radio interview and the Weavers picking a name for themselves right on the air. I can list the names of every famous and slightly famous person who enjoyed the platform of my father's show: Joan Baez, Judy Collins, Dave Van Ronk, Pete Seeger, Woody Guthrie, Bill Monroe, Jean Ritchie, and many others.

But that would be his book. This story is mine.

Left to right: Woody Guthrie, Fred Hellerman, Jean Ritchie, and Pete Seeger waiting to go on Oscar Brand's Folksong Festival. *Late 1940s.*
(Photograph by George Pickow.)

There is a wonderful quote from Dave Van Ronk's book, *The Mayor of MacDougal Street*, co-wrtten with Elijah Wald, where he describes my father as a much-needed mediator between the professional folk musicians who had a platform to play in the clubs and were invited to Town Hall and Carnegie Hall and of course the Festivals, and the "fringe" traditional musicians who weren't yet part of the mainstream and didn't really fit in. He says: "The only place where the two strains crossed was on Oscar Brand's radio show ... . He was incredibly important to the whole scene because for many years his show was the only access the public had to folk music."

Van Ronk also goes on to say: "Oscar knows 575 trillion songs; if any other living human being knew more ... I'd like to see him go toe to toe with Oscar." To prove this point, Dave gives an example anecdote of a drunken night in California, where a friend of Van Ronk's named David Greenhill got into an argument about an arcane point of American History. It was midnight California time – so 3 a.m. New York time. They called Dad to ask the name of Henry Clay's running mate: Oscar, woken out of a sound sleep, burst straight into 'Hurrah! Hurrah! The Country's Risin' for Henry Clay and Frelinghuesen!'"

Van Ronk also notes that Dad managed to "tread a middle ground" between political radicals and more moderate voices in the folk community. "Oscar was one of the few people to have been a steadfast member of the non-Communist Left." One time, Dave writes, he questioned Dad's decision to put Burl Ives on his radio program. Ives had famously cooperated and named names (that of Pete Seeger among them) during his testimony before the House Committee on Un-American Activities (HUAC): Oscar just quietly said, 'Dave, we on the Left do not Blacklist.'" Van Ronk goes on to comment: "[Oscar] put me right in my place."

Although never called to testify, the blacklist nevertheless had a significant negative impact upon his career. Europe eventually provided an escape. He went there with his friend Jean Ritchie and her photographer husband George Pickow.

Dad was introduced to Jean Ritchie by Alan Lomax, the great folklorist and music archivist. He mentioned to my father that there

was this woman who came from Appalachia with a musical instrument most people were unfamiliar with, the dulcimer, and who
knew many songs from her native Kentucky home. Jean was
authentic in every way. Her songs were passed down from generation to generation and traced their roots to England, Scotland, and
Wales. But Jean herself was educated and at that time taught at the
Henry Street Settlement in New York. My father became instantly
intrigued by this smart, unusual musician. He immediately put her
on his show and introduced her to a whole new audience.

Jean Ritchie and Oscar Brand, WNYC Studios, 1947.
(Photograph by George Pickow.)

Her heart always belonged to her husband George. That was a
given. But a special bond grew between my father and Jean that
lasted a lifetime. I think Dad was mesmerized by Jean's total confidence. He always showcased her on his yearly Festival at the Cooper
Union Great Hall, introducing her to the folk community and
people unaccustomed to her unusual brand of traditional music.

So it was this trio – Dad, Jean, and George – who headed on the first of many great adventures abroad. My favorite story, often repeated over Thanksgiving dinner at Jean's house, was the time the threesome rented a tiny car in France and traveled in a dense fog to a special restaurant. Now Dad being the giant man he was, stuffed himself in the back seat, with Jean in the passenger seat and George driving. It was so dark and so foggy that George headed north and followed a bright light up ahead in the distance. All of a sudden the car started making a clunking noise and Jean shouted, "Turn right!" Within seconds they realized they had been on the railroad tracks and were heading straight for an oncoming train. Badly shaken, they decided to stop for some food at a little place shining in the distance. The trio sat down to a big bowl of hot soup. My father looked at the soup, and said to the waiter: "Are you aware that there is an inch of fat floating on my soup?" The waiter answered: "Monsieur, before the war, there were two inches!" Just one of the funny stories that Dad liked to repeat.

The travels with Jean and George forged a friendship that would shape my life as well as my Dad's. No one I ever knew were as close as this trio. While living together in Port Washington, N.Y., overlooking Manhasset Bay, Dad in a basement apartment and Jean and George upstairs, they sailed together and Dad and Jean sang together, recording lovely albums of courting songs, with cover photographs by George.

George did all of Dad's funny, topical album covers. There are a couple of classics, like the skier's album with Dad going off the lift with his pants down around his ankles! Or the car album which shows Dad pumping up the lift to change the tire and the pretty girl in the front seat rising higher and higher in the air. My personal favorite, and it's really hard to pick, has to be *Every Inch a Sailor*. Dad is underwater, dressed as a sailor, with a bikini clad girl behind him as he fences with a swordfish! Classic stuff for the fifties.

So this is the way it worked back then: Jac Holzman of Elektra records would say *We need another theme album.* Let's say, this time for doctors. Dad would write and record 12 songs. Then George would do a funny, clever cover, giant stethoscope looming over a cringing Oscar in his skivvies. You can still find things like this on eBay.

One of the funniest covers was an album of sailing songs. There is a photo of the captain, Dad, holding a martini glass, up to his neck in water, with just the tip of the mast sticking up and his hat askew. This photo was taken in Manhasset Bay, Long Island. Freezing cold that day and cloudy, my father ended up sick with pneumonia. Anything for a laugh. I am thinking now that after all these years it must have been very gratifying for him to see his grandsons fishing off this same dock. I know the walk to town, up the big hill to Jean's house which reminded her of her mountaintop home in Appalachia, and our tall fishing tales, are just part of the continuous love affair I have with that bay, and the community.

Of all the recordings, the most popular are the armed forces albums and of course, *Bawdy Songs.* Many times over the course of my life, but mostly as an adult, I would attend a pub concert, and be enchanted by all the men who came to see Dad sing their favorite songs from the Army or Air Force. Always raising a glass and singing along, as if Dad had actually been with them on their missions.

Special requests meant that the little piece of paper taped to the side of the guitar with his set, the one rehearsed that morning, would generally go the way of the night. Just ask anyone who performed with him as accompanist, like John Foley, or Jonathan Segal. No performance was alike and everyone ended up laughing at the improvised stories or jokes. Especially the performers. Maybe that is why I never got tired of seeing him perform live; he surprised me every time.

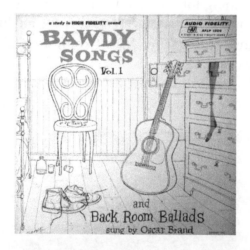

When I grew up and made my own friends, I would find out later that they had listened to the *Bawdy Songs* collection in college. And much to my dismay, they would sing his songs back to me and not always well! In fact, having this happen a number of times, I began to resent the badge that seemed to cling to me. I am very proud of all of Dad's accomplishments, and he never, ever swore at home, or told risqué stories. In fact, being polite was part of our upbringing, so you can imagine how this felt. Somehow it was unseemly, and so now I am the epitome of politeness and good breeding, to the point of being made fun of as the "prim and proper" Miss Jeannie.

When Jean and George started their own little family, it was time for my father to take his next step too. He returned briefly to Canada. But my father wanted to live in the U.S. He wrote a song for Doris Day, called "A Guy is a Guy." When it made the hit parade and Dad finally had some real income, he decided it was time to come back and settle down. When he was invited on the Kate Smith T.V. show, it was the equivalent of a U.S. stamp of approval. It was 1955 and he was 35 years old.

Much later, in the early sixties, Dad took a job hosting a show in Canada called *Let's Sing Out!* It benefited most of his friends who could not find work in the U.S. Many artists remained blacklisted, so the opportunity to perform on Dad's show was a great gift. In fact, to this day I still come across many misinformed people who still believe that Dad was at the very least sympathetic to the Communist Party. But in actuality, in those days it was really guilt by association, and folk music was rapidly changing from traditional to anthem. But in Canada, tradition reigned and so did Oscar Brand. (Many of the people he introduced on his Canadian show became famous in America. Joni Anderson [Mitchell] and Gordon Lightfoot come to mind.)

In Canada, my father eventually became a big star. A "mobbed at the airport" kind of star. Because he had written a song called "Something to Sing About," which almost became the Canadian National Anthem, and is certainly still thought of today as the country's "unofficial" anthem.

And now it's my story. Well, actually, not yet. But almost.

My father fell in love with a 20 year old June Taylor dancer on the Jackie Gleason Show. This young, Audrey Hepburn look-alike was an ex- Rockette, and a child star, performing on Broadway at the age of four in "Annie Get Your Gun," with Ethel Merman. Also a ballerina and flamenco dancer. Do I really need to add that she had a driven backstage mother who was a severe disciplinarian and sought to make up for her orphaned childhood and losing a baby son to polio by turning her only daughter into a puppet of her forceful will? I am guessing, though I do not know for sure, that marriage was a good way out of this life for my mother. She accepted my father's proposal and they were married in 1955.

Their huge wedding was filmed by George Pickow, who eventually filmed my wedding as well. Of course, you never see George, because he was behind the camera; but there are a great many stunning close-ups of Jean, my godmother for whom I was named, with her flaming red hair and beautiful bright green dress. (I should note, by the way, that few besides my parents and Jean seem to be smiling at this glossy, overblown, floral extravaganza.)

The newlyweds moved into an apartment on West 12th Street, neighbors with my Dad's accompanist and his partner, who would later become my godfather. The good kind of godfather. The kind who bought a motherless girl her first Tiffany gift, a trip to F.A.O. Schwarz on my birthday, a *Bon Voyage* party on the QE2! Mostly, the kind of godfather who makes a fuss about a little girl just because she is special to him. He even installed an ice cream parlor in his apartment. Coming over for special treats was such a delight – the dreaded and forbidden maraschino cherry available in abundance! Dinner out for a special occasion at Fedora's in the Village was a great treat, mostly because it was an artistic crowd and very accepting of all lifestyles.

This is something I never thought much about until recently. Openly gay, Dick moved away when I was very young, heading to the West Coast, fleeing the prejudice of his family. But we keep in contact, never forgetting a birthday, and sharing special memories.

Recently, I watched this 16mm wedding movie, long hidden away, with a perverse eye towards remembering something positive from my childhood. You see, by now, it's been 45 plus years since I've seen my mother, and one of my nephews is interested in our family tree. I thought I would send him a copy in DVD form and be done with it. But it turns out, there was so much more on that tape.

Chapter Two

My guess is that my father spliced these many films together at some point.

Let's start with the first thing I saw besides the wedding and honeymoon. My mother, nine months pregnant in a silver maternity dress with dangling earrings, full makeup and hair done up, walks into the room with a bag of knitting. No sound. Next scene: She makes exactly the same entrance and begins to knit – thus raising the suspicion that this is staged. Which it was.

Actually, all the scenes for the next 8 years were staged. My father used to tell me that he knew on his honeymoon that marrying my mother was a mistake. I believe that is a difficult thing for any child to hear, especially when it means I wouldn't exist, but apparently it was true. However, by then I was already *on the way*, as they used to say.

Few people can actually say they have a recording of the night they were born. Apparently, Dad was doing a concert with Bob Abramson accompanying him while at the same time, unbeknownst to him, my mother walked through the snow with Jean Ritchie to the New York Infirmary. Word of my birth got to Bob somehow before it got to Dad. After being tipped off by Bob, the audience – at his signal – broke into a chorus of "Happy Birthday" while Dad was in the middle of another song. You can hear it on the tape. Then laughter and applause, as Dad finished the concert.

Back at the hospital another drama took place. While my mother was still unconscious, my maternal grandmother arrived and put my name on the birth certificate as *Naomi*. This was the birth name of her sister who had rescued her from the orphanage where she had been dropped off with a younger brother who later died there.

Many tragic stories of immigrants started with a parent who

didn't speak English, looking for work, and thinking that an orphanage was a good way to have their children fed and cared for – although most, like my great-grandfather, were never heard from again.

When my grandmother's beloved sister came from Romania, they asked her at Ellis Island for her name; all she could answer in English was *Moldavia, Romania*. So they put her name down on the record as *Molly*, and her birth-name of *Naomi* became nothing but a memory. Grandma wanted a fitting tribute to her sister, and a little girl named *Naomi* would be just the way to show her devotion; plus in the Jewish faith, that's the way it was done, to remember those who had passed and sacrificed for us.

Yes. Naming me *Naomi* would be a fitting tribute, but *Naomi* was not the name that was supposed to be given. My name was promptly changed to *Jeannie*, after Jean Ritchie, my Godmother. My "Hebrew" name, which I've never used, remained *Naomi*. Everyone happy? No. My mother stopped talking to her mother after that.

I know a few things about my very early childhood. I know my father adored me. I know I had lots of exposure to loving people who cared for me; in fact my first word was *Murray*, because a best buddy of my father lived close by and visited often. Later Murray Lerner would make a film called "Festival" about the Newport Folk Festival. (My father was part of the original board of directors along with Theo Bikel, Pete Seeger, George Wein, and Albert Grossman.) This very famous film, on which George Pickow served as cinematographer, showcases early talent and the movement of folk music towards the mainstream.

Years later, when I was watching the Academy Awards in 1969, a man received the Best Documentary Oscar for a film called "From Mao to Mozart," and it was Murray! My Murray! I remember at the time shouting out *Hey, I know that guy*; but I say that a lot. People became famous and I remember them from dinner parties, Seders, the radio broadcast, and television. But from a perspective of recognizing childhood characters that came and went through our home and our lives, not just stories.

Now the mystery begins. Most women don't go on a holiday after they have a baby. Apparently, this was the norm for my mother. The reason for a European tour for my mother is unclear. Maybe post-partum depression. What I do know is that my father came home to me sleeping in the bottom drawer of a bureau. My crying was annoying my mother, and they decided she needed a break. She went to visit her flamenco dance partner in Barcelona, and I became the baby who always needed a sitter. I wound up with a famous one.

Daddy's Girl, 1959. (Brand Family Collection.)

With a great deal of people around to help in a pinch, my father had his choice of babysitters. Nannies didn't become part of the plan until my second brother was born. It just seemed to be unseemly for a folksinger to be able to afford a nanny. And besides, that was never a part of my father's frame of reference. Family took care of their own. A mother with no instinct for caring was a huge surprise I'm sure, so he turned to friends and neighbors.

Eleanor Roosevelt had an apartment near where we lived in the Village. When Mrs. Roosevelt needed Dad to perform at one of her many fundraisers, a benefit concert, he explained it would be his pleasure. He just had one little problem: *me*. No problem. Mrs. Roosevelt volunteered to take care of me. Mrs. Roosevelt had always been a good friend to folk music. She and the President had invited many artists to the White House, including Josh White, a black musician. Many years later, my father would tour with his son, Josh White, Jr., and Odetta. A special trio, with lots of history and all managed by close friend Doug Yeager.

On this particular occasion, Dad dropped me off only to return hours later to find me screaming and crying. (I cried a lot, apparently; still do.) He asked Mrs. Roosevelt if this was a problem. She graciously replied "No, I just turned off my hearing aid!" So, under those circumstances, when the need arose again, Mrs. Roosevelt stepped in. I understand later she had to stop, because her own children complained that she didn't babysit for them. Well maybe she just got a little more from taking care of me.

I heard that many years later, when she was asked about the Blacklist, she replied that they would have come after her too, if she hadn't once been First Lady. I still like and admire her to this day. Many people found her difficult and not warm to family; but knowing her history, basically ignored and taunted by her mother and humiliated by her mother-in-law, I'd say she had a right to her peculiarities.

No other First Lady accomplished so much, both during and after her unprecedented time in the White House. No argument there. When they built the monument to President Franklin Roosevelt, they also made a statue of Eleanor. The only First Lady to have that honor. I remember visiting this memorial and having my photograph taken in front of it. The statue towered over me. I sent the photo to my father.

Most children have very few memories of their really early life. Since most memories are documented by family members, we absorb them and they become our own. I have nothing before my brother arrived. But in the tradition of our mother, and with no clue as to why my father and mother stayed together, mother needed another "getaway" after my brother was born.

Divorce was a bigger deal, and far more rare, in those days than it is now. And if it did take place, no father would receive custody. But my father actually feared for our lives. My mother grew up enduring extreme punishment and cruelty. Some people escape their pasts by trying new behavior, not repeating it. Still, I never understood why my folks stayed together – although I truly believe that the alternative might have been worse in my father's mind. And he was right.

Recently, a friend was reading *Positively 4ᵗʰ Street* by David Hajdu, and she came upon a cute story of the first appearance of Joan Baez at the Newport Folk Festival in 1960. Apparently, Joan was 18 at the time and virtually unknown outside of the Boston area. She asked George Wein if she could join Bob Gibson onstage for part of his set. George answered that Oscar Brand was the M.C. and it would be up to him. The schedule was tight, but my father said if Bob was willing to give up part of his 12 minutes, then it was fine with him. My one year old brother, Eric, was asleep backstage when Joan began to sing. Her high pitched remarkable voice was enough to wake him, at which point he joined in with a loud crying voice of his own! There are lots of stories like that in Hadju's book, and it proves to me that we were there very early on. Dad never left us behind if possible; but since I don't actually remember these early gems, I will stick to what I know.

So here's all I remember about those early years: lots of music and laughter, the children put to bed early so the friends could drink and jam, guests staying over, lots of peaking and giggling to the point where my father had to put gates on our beds, to prevent us from mingling with the folk-set. But we saw it all.

After a night of partying, Dad was off to work, but Mom slept in. Dad never touched a drink, but Mom made up for it. She slept VERY late. In order to have anything to eat, I learned how to cook eggs on the stove for my brother and myself. He was two; I was six; and that was about it. Thank you Dr. Seuss and *Green Eggs and Ham*. The only way I convinced my brother to eat was to read the book to him. We were very close, and still are.

1961: Eric (2) and Jeannie (6).
(Brand Family Collection.)

Weekend excursions to Jean and George's house were a highlight. I think we had a Ford Falcon station wagon, which we kept at the gas station around the corner in the Village. Always concerned with our safety, my father put a huge mattress in the back and my brother and I would lay down, supposedly to nap on the way. Instead we watched the telephone poles whizz by and generally tortured each other. Maybe this is when the sing-a-longs started, to keep us quiet and in line.

In Port Washington we cavorted with Peter and Jon Pickow, and played games and listened to music. Always good food and music. Jean had such a big house. People from all over the world that she met in her travelling would stop and stay. Sometimes a week, sometimes months.

I sat at the feet of Doc Watson who regaled us with stories of his youth. The kids and I were more interested in the Monopoly game we were playing, but Doc just kept talking. We listened to rounds of songs and square danced in the big living room. The fireplace in the big room was so huge that you could stand in it! There was also a loft office for Jean overhanging the big room, from which sleepy children could just watch as festivities lasted into the wee hours.

The room was decorated with memorabilia from concerts, posters, and a few pieces of artwork from local artists, some of whom became famous later. (In fact, there was an artist named Frank Kleinholz – whom *Newsweek* would eventually call "a Brooklyn-born Gauguin" – who had done a family portrait of the Pickows, which hung in a major place of honor in their big room. I remember Frank because he was rebuilding his home in Port Washington, and all the kids were invited to "help" by pulling old nails out of the wood. He rewarded us with sketches and paintings which he inscribed to us, and which I still have to this day.) But it was the way the Pickows' artwork was displayed that was most intriguing. George and Jean just hung things up in the order in which they acquired them; so some overlapped and some were crooked, which was in stark contrast to the artwork in our house which was always perfectly balanced. Many of George's own paintings also hung all about the house.

Most of the time my brother and I would end up staying over in Peter's room, using sleeping bags. Of course, we didn't sleep much – cousins and friends talking and laughing all night long.

I always marveled at Jean's big Christmas tree in the smaller parlor living room. It had real angels made of corn husks, which the Ritchie family were famous for in the Appalachians, and I have a lovely collection today. The tree also had real candles. Every year

Jean would sit in the rocker by the tree and close her eyes, as if remembering the Christmases of her mountain youth. Her father's portrait hung over the mantle. It was warm, cozy, and inviting. I loved it.

I would very much like to say that this was the happiest time of my life. But as much as I love and respect my godmother, I need to say that since my mother wasn't around for these occasions, I was still caregiver, so I was responsible for my brother. No nonsense Jean had her own kids. She made this very clear. When my brother stepped in dog poo, it was my responsibility to clean it up. Or when getting ready for the great toboggan races down the deep tree lined hill, I was responsible for getting my brother and I bundled up and not getting us killed!

Later, when I was in my twenties, Jean and I became very close. I lived in the Pickows' basement apartment until I got married. The same basement Alan Lomax had lived in for a time. But the early years were difficult, because I really needed a role model.

By now, with Dad trying to develop new avenues of his career (television, Broadway, concerts, touring), my mother wanted her own time to shine once more. She couldn't stand the heat of NYC in the summer and decided a move to the country might help. I know she really campaigned for this. To appease her temporarily, Dad rented a penthouse apartment on West 12th Street, complete with a walk-out patio for gardening. About as close to the country as we were going to get, for now.

I know my father loved the city and especially Sundays, when you could find us dancing under the sprinkling water of Washington Square Park. We splashed around while Dad recorded the music being played by folkies nearby in the park, and interviewed people using his very sophisticated "Portable" tape recorder. Then a quick dash to WNYC for a live broadcast with whoever was around.

WNYC, our home away from home. On a Sunday night it was completely empty, so my brother and I would play in the halls. Freshly waxed floors for racing and sliding, also sneaking to the rooftop and hanging from the Gargoyles over NYC with only belt loops preventing my brother from taking a dive! How we survived? Just dumb luck. There was also a wonderful library for the archives run by an old man who always kept a select candy reward just for Oscar's kids. We used the typewriters in everyone's offices and spun in their chairs until dizzy. No one knew. There was only one rule. Dad was on the air, so be quiet and stay alive.

Once at Washington Square, after becoming bored with the fountain, Eric and I went over to the swings and slide. When he came down the slide head first into the pavement and cut open his chin, everyone looked around for his mother. I was crying. Dad was recording and singing. Oblivious. Someone called an ambulance and away Eric went!

When Dad came looking for us I was pretty hysterical. I'd been told never to move from the spot last seen, to make it easier to find us if we were lost. So I just stood there. Through my tears, I managed to explain, and we located my pretty shaken little brother at the St. Vincent's Hospital emergency room. He still has the scar and I still have the memory; so after that I became pretty strict with my babysitting efforts.

One of my favorite things was heading over the Brooklyn Bridge for dinner at Grandma Bea's apartment. Grandma Bea, or GG as she was known to her many grandchildren, was a truly classic character. Once a beauty queen, a serious head-on accident with a truck had left her beautiful face damaged. I have seen photos of her in her youth posing in parades, and raising money for the veterans of the First World War – but I only knew her as older, with a gravelly voice from smoking all her life and a real adoration for her son, who was on the radio.

Grandma was a real dame: a poker playing sales gal, with opinions about everything. My father's father had passed away when I was about five, so most of my memories are of this special time alone with GG. We watched *Jeopardy* together and shouted the answers at the T.V. On special occasions, my father would take Eric home after dinner and I was allowed to sleep over.

There were strict orders from my mother, not to give me the *three* Cs: cola, coffee, or cereal. Of course, grandma gave me anything I wanted. Mom being a drunk didn't fit in with her health conscience concern for my welfare, and GG took no orders from her. I didn't get much sleep because GG snored, but the big feather bed and the attention was enough to make this a very special night off.

By this time I had started school in the Village at P.S. 41. It was a couple of blocks from home and even kids as young as I walked alone then. Every shopkeeper knew you and your routine. Every doorman said *hello*. No fear of anything except recess and the concrete if you fell and skinned your knee, because girls all wore dresses to school.

There was a wonderful fruit stand on Greenwich Avenue where a Mrs. Balducci always had a fresh flower or apple to hand me as I passed by on my way home. Now, fifty years later, Balducci's is an upscale supermarket, franchised nationwide. Not one person I talked to on their opening day in Washington, D.C. had any knowledge of the humble beginnings of the store. But I do, and I will never forget Mrs. B's kindness; so I shop there *just because*.

I also loved the new penthouse we had moved to. It was close to school and bright and airy. Decorated with so many plants and sunlight, Jon Vie bakery around the corner. Dad was doing well. For the moment Mom seemed happy.

Besides the Newport Folk Festival, and various others, including the Philadelphia Folk Festival and the Mariposa Festival in Toronto, our summers were spent at a Catskills resort called *Grossinger's*. Jenny Grossinger was a fan of folk music, and Jerry Hirschman and Dad put together a wonderful program of musicians and comedians to attract the city dwellers for a few weeks at the hotel. It was really a great idea. Family entertainment, workshops for the kids, and programs of a more adult nature at night. We had our own table in the dining room and everyone knew Oscar's kids. My brother and I had free reign during the day and would sit by the pool or go to Dad's children's parties. For many years a photograph of the family hung on the wall there, right next to that of Theo Bikel.

I loved Grossinger's for the freedom I tasted for the first time, as I snuck out one night to hear Jackie Mason, the comedian. Thinking I would never get caught since Dad and Mom had a separate room, I sat down somewhere in the audience and don't you know, Jackie Mason saw me! He pointed me out in the audience and a giant spotlight hit my face as he shouted: "What are you doing up so late?" Sounds silly, but I was so mortified that I ended up disliking him and his humor for the next 40 or so years, until I finally went to see him again in concert, as a gesture of forgiveness, which of course he was not aware of at all. He was still acerbic and insulting, except this time it wasn't directed specifically at me.

The other neat thing about this resort was its swimming pool. Not the outdoor one, which Dad liked to hang out at and receive his fans informally, but the indoor pool, because it boasted a glass window in the game room. I was absolutely fascinated by the look of bobbing people from their underside. Many years later, I returned to see the resort in disrepair and falling apart, but the funny underwater window still existed, except no one was swimming in the long forgotten indoor pool.

A while ago, I was speaking to my step-mother, who was just a teenage girl at the time when she visited Grossinger's to see my father with her friends. She casually mentioned that she had seen me and my brother there. How very disturbing this is to think about. Nice that she had been a fan so early on, but really odd, since my parents were still together and it was just my brother and me at that point in time. I asked her if she introduced herself to my father as a fan might. He is very approachable, always was – that was the way of the relaxed atmosphere at the resort. But she said no, he was with his family and she didn't want to interrupt. I keep thinking how strange this was, and I must confess, a little unsettling, since eventually this teenager would grow up and marry him.

The best thing for me to do is to forget this knowledge for now. There were many encounters between my father and his fans. I am well aware of this; it was and still remains something of an entertainment industry fundamental. Especially in those days. Television was a young medium and people who were famous were like a magnet in person. My father has terrific charisma. I used to say he sucked all the air out of the room when he entered. But that wasn't an insult; it was a compliment. He seemed larger than life and always at the center of everything he did.

I figured out long ago that when he earned the moniker of "Oscar the Grouch" by Jim Henson, who worked with Dad on the Board of the Children's Television Workshop, it was for a reason. Dad fought for a show with relatable scenery for inner city kids. A neighborhood complete with people of color, garbage cans on the street and trash. Hence the Muppet, no royalties, good family story.

Recently, I became aware that after 45 years, *Sesame Street* has been sold to HBO. I haven't had a sighting of Oscar the Grouch for a while, so I guess his character did not sign on for this new gig. And for some reason, completely unexplained, Kermit and Miss Piggy are getting a divorce. Sounds ridiculous to be concerned, but shouldn't the message be that some people stay together? Maybe this too is more relatable to children, since the divorce rate is so high. (Could have been the interspecies thing, but not my call.)

My father had many life lessons that he would impart to me. He would proclaim them out of nowhere, just because it occurred to him at that moment. My all-time favorite has to be: "Don't expect people to act on information they don't have." Classic, and true and I definitely use this advice. Seems straightforward enough, but so many of us go under the assumption that everybody knows everything already.

The other perfect gift of advice, which I think could only come from a performer father, was to remember to always enter a room as if the most important person in the world has just arrived. Then make sure you leave early. Also, of course, always be on time and bring your guitar. Well, I can do two out of three. Habitually early and trying to keep everyone entertained and happy to this day.

Then there was that wonderful annual ritual: the Newport Folk Festival: Early years spent enjoying the children's programs during the day and shuffling around bored at night, having no clue about the famous and infamous people we were getting drinks or sand-wiches for.

I remember being in one foot of a gigantic Bread and Puppet Theater creation during a children's performance. My brother was in the other foot. Two steps forward and one step back made the giant puppet look like it was walking! We sometimes sang with my Dad at a daytime children's workshop onstage. Night was very different, because the "big" stars came out.

Some people actually scared me. When Doug Kershaw in a tight fitting purple velvet suit started playing, all I saw was the suit. He was very young and very excited to be there. Enough said, but I remember it to this day.

The biggest crisis now seems funny, and indeed it's become a family joke, but one night Janis Joplin was singing with her group "Big Brother and the Holding Company." She was really into the song and started to strip off her clothes. Dad instructed me to take my brother back to the large mansion that had been rented for the performers to stay in. I said, "Why Dad? Her boobs are already out!" Still, he was adamant; so I climbed into the shuttle car.

My brother sat on Sonny Terry's lap. I was squished in the back with Ramblin' Jack Elliott and his wife. Brownie McGhee, also in front, was yelling and fighting with Jack Elliott who was upset that his wife was not feeling great. She was nursing a baby at the time. I was mortified that everyone around us was yelling. It was loud in that car that night. But back at our room, we were sung to sleep by those lovely men, Sonny and Brownie. The whole house was alive with music and everyone always looked out for Oscar's kids.

Much, much later, that little baby in the back seat of that car grew up and produced a scathing documentary called "The Ballad of Ramblin' Jack," about her father's drinking and his being on the road all the time. Dad and I joked that I could never write a tell-all book, because I didn't have a good enough story. No skeletons or abuse, and he never drank or took drugs. Very funny Dad. Believe me, there is plenty to write about.

There are so many stories about Newport and the summer festivals in general, and I promise to get to them. My adventures really started at later festivals, when I was older and in charge of everyone's kids. I remember one morning when my little brother Eric got stuck in a port-a-potty and we couldn't open the door! I was frantic, and I looked around for a grown-up to help. A very big, tall man came along and I cried that my brother was stuck. Well, he muscled up his strength and pulled the door clean off the hinge. That nice man was Johnny Cash.

Once returned to the city, we fell back into the routine of family life. This doesn't mean we had structure at home. It just means that we had a base. A place we called *home*. Dinner waiting at a specific time. No A&W rest stops on the way to another festival. No reason to hop in the car for eight hours and sing eighteen verses of "Jenny Jenkins" to make time pass. Seriously, how many kids were taught Irish campaign songs to sing in the car? We didn't even know what half the words meant, but they rhymed and were funny, so we sang them.

During the school year, in the beginning, Dad was home most nights. I am sure now that this was just an illusion for us kids, because so much has been written about his coffee house days and all the talent he played with, but we were asleep by then, so there was definitely a feeling at least of a schedule. Concerts followed on weekends, when he also did most of his interviews and edited his radio broadcast. (On Sunday mornings he sometimes appeared on the popular kids' television show "Wonderama," with host, Sonny Fox, and we kept the toys they advertised, so that was a special treat.)

My earliest memory of the penthouse at 79 West 12th street is the sweetie pie doorman, who looked out for us when we played in the street or rode our bikes. Also the weekly visit to the A&P across the street, where I was absolutely mortified that my father would ride the cart down the aisles, whistling and singing. I pretended not to know him. How absurd. I should have wondered why he was food shopping in the first place. I guess that sounds sexist, but it was the sixties. What exactly was my mother doing? I would soon find out.

This was the first of many times that my world would be ripped out from under me. First grade is so important because friendships are made and you develop a taste of how you will fare in the big world outside. I made friends quickly and was very happy. So, of course, following first grade and a summer spent at a camp called Mount Tom, my brother and I did *not* go home to the apartment on West 12th in the Village, and I did not go back to the school and friends I'd come to know so well.

Instead, we landed at our new home in Croton, NY, in the Hudson Valley: a thirteen acre estate with an orchard, also a wine cellar, dog run, lake … and a history.

Chapter Three

Apparently, the bottom of this great house had been a Revolutionary War fort that was entirely made of stone, with the house being built around it. Also, it had the strange distinction of being haunted by the previous owner, a local story, and one my mother dragged out to keep us in line when necessary. A few closets that led to other rooms, which was fun for spying on the grown-ups, or running away, depending on the mood of the day. The house leaked so badly that our rooms – in the basement, far from the folks on the third floor – would constantly flood. So in deference to our beds floating every once in a while, we also had a shared room on the first floor. The reason for the big move to the country, was really to entertain. Pete Seeger, one of dad's closest friends, lived just up the pike in Beacon, N.Y., in a log cabin he built with his own hands. No inside plumbing at first.

The "Oscar Brand House" as it was later named by the residents of Croton, was located behind the elementary school about a quarter mile down a long secluded driveway. You would never know a house was there. Just a dirt path and tangled trees. No one would ever wander there alone and the mailbox was located several blocks away, on a corner near the end of the school street.

The house itself boasted a huge kitchen, maid's quarters and butler bells, but the main attraction was the second floor living room, which was really three living rooms. Reminded me of the ballrooms you see in the movies, but this one had a fireplace at the end and three complete rooms of furniture for company. The children were never allowed on the second floor unless there was a party. That was the adults' domain. We children remained segregated unless there were guests. And there were guests. This was how my father decided to keep my mother happy. It lasted three years.

I am having a very difficult time trying to get beyond this last sentence. I haven't written a decent word in three months. I know that now the memories will be very real and very painful, because now I know the truth.

I wrote that these were the happiest years of my life. I'm not sure as an adult how I can believe that I actually think that way, because looking back, so much took place that changed the trajectory of our lives in a small space of time. Watching the footage of that film. I see a little happy family playing with a dog on the lawn at Croton, not realizing that a giant meteor was about to come flaming straight towards them. We never saw it coming.

Jeannie's 7ᵗʰ Birthday. Croton, 1963.
(Brand Family Collection.)

The years we lived in Croton were 1963-1965. Just take a moment to think about those years. What they meant to you, if you lived at that time. What they meant to the country. What happened historically, of course, had an impact on everyone. We were no different, except that for those who were political, or wanted to make a better world through peace and a song, things were changing fast. And not in a good way.

Memories flood in on me. Are you interested in the perspective of a seven year old girl? Or in the famous people who came and camped out at our house and partied and collaborated and debated our changing America? I know the answer: *Come on, name some people, and keep me interested.* I have heard this all my life. Who do you know? Tell me a story no one knows. Okay I promise. But first you're going to hear about how it feels to grow up thinking this is normal.

My very first memories of the big house are the cats and dogs. Seriously, we never had pets in the city. But in the country every cat had kittens and they stayed. None were ever allowed in the house, but there was plenty to catch in the woods to eat, and a pond for water. Looking back, I guess my mother treated the animals much like she did us. Self-sufficient. If you survived until morning, she'd done her job.

Actually, several people did her job.

There was a housekeeper, Mrs. Dickie. And a couple who stayed rent free in exchange for babysitting, Pamela and Bumper; his real name, from England. Later on there came a nanny, in a separate wing, for a new baby.

Right from the start my mother told us the house was haunted by the ghost of Mr. Pomeroy. If we ever misbehaved, he would take care of disciplining us. So basically, I was pretty afraid of my own home. Now I know this doesn't exactly sound like the happiest years of my life, but I made a lot of friends; and I spent most of my time sleeping over at their houses when my father traveled. So in my own little girl way, I had the best of both worlds.

A non-participating mother is hard to miss when she is never seen. In fact, sometimes my friends' mothers would take me shopping for clothes. Truly a gesture of kindness, probably because I had great manners, and it guaranteed an invite to the next party at the Brands'.

Then there was the dog. *DYLAN*. (I didn't make the connection then.) This Welsh Corgi was my father's dog in every sense and treated me like the enemy. The dog was so vicious that one of my earliest memories is of being terrorized by him as I bicycled home from a friend's house, the dog nipping my feet the whole way, protecting his master, who wasn't even home. Many times I would have to call from a neighbor's house to make sure someone was holding him before I would even consider walking home alone down my own driveway. I recently asked my father who gave him this dog? He said a "fan."

With my father, you never really know what he means. Either joking or serious, there is always a point or a lesson. This was just after Bob Dylan had gone, "electric' at Newport. The stories are legendary about Bob being booed, and the established generation unwilling to accept any change.

But Dad's opinion really was the best. Dad believed that night was not the "end" of Folk Music. Traditional music always morphs into the current sound. People were upset, yes, but if you listen to how close the anthems were, it really doesn't matter which instrument they were played on. The important thing was the message.

Not long after that infamous night at Newport, Dad visited Woody Guthrie in the hospital; they both had a good laugh over it. Little Bobby Dylan goes electric. This was funny to them, because he had originally come to New York to worship at the feet of Guthrie, making up all sorts of stories about a Carnival past and hitching ride on freight trains. Just listen to Bob's first radio broadcast which is archived from my father's show, where he tells these outrageous stories. And now here he was finding his own voice, a considerable one granted, but just funny to two old friends who had been there since the beginning.

Many years later, on his 70th anniversary radio broadcast, at 95 years old, Dad played Billy Joel's "We didn't Start the Fire." Just a perfect answer to the people who thought change was offensive and would ruin tradition. Folk music was, is, and always will be the music of the people – no matter the style.

Back to the dogs, which is how I got on the Dylan track. Occasionally, they did stroll into the house. Not often, and not with company there. But after the big "flea" infestation, I never saw them inside again. *Yes, I do refer to two dogs here, but the second is part of a juicy story to come later.*

By now the Thanksgiving parties were being hosted in Croton and recorded by my father for his radio broadcast. The parties were legendary. Jean Ritchie owned Christmas, but the parties at Oscar's house in Croton were the place to be on Thanksgiving and most weekends. There seemed to always be a Hootenanny, and it was pretty much an open house. With plenty of room to spend the night, or come and go as you pleased, most parties lasted at least three days. Upstairs in the big room, Dad made the rounds with his microphone, while some of the most unlikely people swapped their versions of songs and music handed down from generation to generation.

This was all for fun, not for anyone's entertainment except for themselves (and often the listeners of WNYC). No pressure, no rehearsal, just good food and good company.

There is a particularly funny recording of a group which included Jean Ritchie, Roger Sprung, Doc Watson, Ralph Rinzler, John Cohen, and Mike Seeger, and one of the Clancy Brothers, trying to finish just one song to be used on the broadcast. Everyone keeps laughing and breaking up and you can hear Dad saying come on guys, this is for the radio, deadly serious, and then he breaks up laughing too. He plays this recording every Thanksgiving, so I know it reminds him of those wonderful gatherings too.

Now imagine the food. Everyone brought guests or family. How did we manage the food? This is my most vivid memory because I was the runner from the big kitchen to upstairs, platters of

hot food from the gigantic oven. Now remember this was an extremely old house and even boasted kerosene lamps that pulled
down from the ceiling and worked, so when I tell you that after
three days of constant cooking the oven blew up and the door came
crashing through into the hallway, taking tiles off the walls with it,
you can believe me.

Most people in Croton were so proud of their new-fangled
electric kitchens. But when the big blackout of 1964 hit New York, it
was to our house that all the neighbors flocked. The kids played all-
night monopoly games and tried to stay awake. No one seemed
scared because there was a place to go. The Brand house. Always
open. Come on over.

Jean Ritchie and Oscar playing badminton, Croton, 1964.
(Photograph by George Pickow.)

In those days, Croton and the immediate region around Croton
was a mecca for a lot of artists: the folklorist Ben Botkin, John
Cheever, Joseph Heller, Andy Warhol, Gloria Swanson, and our
friend Eleanor Roosevelt. But the fact that Lee Hays of the Weavers

had retired there was a good reason to live in Croton specifically. Later I learned that Jackie Gleason also kept a house nearby. That would have enticed my mother, who had been on his T.V. show. I remember making friends with a girl in my class named Judy Bernz, and just by coincidence, it was her property that leased the guest house to Lee Hays. We visited often. The house was on top of a very steep hill called Mount Airy Road.

It's funny, because at the time I didn't understand why my father would bother to come on a playdate with me. I thought he'd just drive me and pick me up later. Now I know his good friend Lee was there and in a wheelchair by then. He was part of the family of folksingers who visited each other and still always respected each other long after they were able to perform or come down the mountain to visit us.

A favorite memory of the Croton period, was a unique visit to Fred Hellerman's house in Weston, Connecticut. Unique because after the Weavers broke up, he didn't make many public appearances. But also because he had this amazing room in his house. I'll never forget it or the story that follows, because it is part of the Brand "secret treasured story collection."

As near as I can remember, Freddy took us to this room filled with all the latest recording equipment. It was laid out like a giant banquet on several tables with levers and all sorts of speakers. Now Dad's recording for his broadcast had always either swung on his shoulders at an interview, or fit into a closet, reel to reel, so little hands wouldn't touch. This was an enormous display. Freddy was so proud at the ability to over dub or run two or more tracks at the same time. He invited us to listen to an African chant that he had just recorded. We listened enraptured by all the voices slowly joining in and mixing together.

The lyric sounded like, "Petzy, Gamash U Ga." Over and over, until the room broke up laughing, because it was actually "Pete Seeger, mashugah." Which is a Yiddish expression for "pain in the ass." To this day, when Dad plays it on his radio show, he never gives away the "secret" until the end of the chant. Funny and telling at the same time.

This is a perfect time to revisit an old friend and story about my father which has nothing to do with Croton, but everything to do with old friends. Sometimes it comes up in a conversation or a book, but I know this story from the lips of my father, so I am sure it is true. When Woody Guthrie was hospitalized with Huntington's Chorea, his family would pay him visits. I know this from many stories Arlo would tell. What is little known, as I have previously referred to, is that Dad also visited, always with a box of Whitman Chocolates, Woody's favorite, and a clean shirt or other "necessities." Dad also sent monthly checks to Woody.

Now I know that Woody Guthrie is a very famous man. But at the time, he had children to support, I believe seven in all, and his care was costly. I just thought you ought to know about Dad's part. He was not only a great friend to many, but he used his resources to make sure everyone he knew that needed help had it.

Recently, I joined a Facebook group open only to people who had actually lived in Croton during the sixties. The brother of a childhood friend had sponsored my membership in this little closed group, so I posted who I was and asked if anyone had memories of me as a child. Well of course I got close to 140 responses, two of them about me and the rest about my father. But actually, I am realizing now as I write that this is going to continue to happen and that it is okay. Our lives were so closely intertwined, especially after my mother ran away and I have to embrace that and not deny that this story, although completely mine, is my father's story too.

There were many memories of Dad performing at the local schools and inviting kids over to the house for music and delightful parties. Someone reminded me of a crazy car that my father bought abroad, which wasn't even legal in the U.S. because it was so light.

It was called a *Deux Cheveaux*. The top rolled back like a sardine can and the windows folded up. We stood on the backseat, made of canvas and stretched rubber bands, heads sticking out of the top, going down to the Silver Lake. Everyone seemed to remember this car: an upside-down bathtub, later to become part of our clubhouse in the woods. There exists a photo of my mother hauling a giant antique Grandfather clock in that little car. She has to sit on the front of the car, just to keep it from tipping over. The next time I would see a car like it was fifty years later, in Washington, D.C. at the Hillwood Estate of Marjorie Merriweather Post.

But of course, on that Facebook thread, there were also the people who after all these years could not contain themselves, and had to give their opinion of folk music as a whole, and believe the local gossip from that time, still distancing themselves from our family because all folksingers were Communists. Really? Still? Just makes me crazy.

Recently, a good friend to our family – the distinguished journalist, Frank Beacham – wrote a beautiful essay about my father on the occasion of my Dad's 96th birthday. He eloquently explained that the WNYC program was a platform for so many artists that had been blacklisted, or had Leftist leanings, and since Dad was never paid for the show, he had nothing to lose financially and was able to give a voice to everyone who came and had something to sing about. That is why my father was listed in the infamous unofficial "directory" of the blacklist, "Red Channels." Not because he was ever a member of the Communist Party, but because his show was called a "pipeline to Communism" by dint of actually NOT blacklisting anyone who wanted to appear. And of course after 70 plus years, it feels good to finally put that chapter to rest.

The only supermarket in town in those days was a Grand Union. There was a tiny strip mall that also had a Post Office as I recall. My memory of the GU, as we used to call it, was the once-a-week shopping trip. My folks did this together. The only time I can remember that they did anything together. My brother and I climbed in the back of the station wagon and they drove away. On this particular day, after loading the groceries and my little brother, off they went. I was still riding the little steel horse ride in front! I didn't panic at all, and apparently they didn't miss me, because they didn't turn around. I walked over to the post office and said: *I think my parents just forgot me.*

The nice man behind the desk asked my name and address. I didn't know my address but I told him my father's name. He knew exactly where I lived and either called my father or took me home, I can't remember. Nowadays they probably would call child protective services. Back then Dad autographed an album as a *thank-you* and everybody had a good laugh. Maybe that's when I started looking after myself. It wasn't going to be the last time I was left stranded. But it was the last time there was a happy ending.

Eric in the Deux Cheveaux, Croton, 1964.
(Brand Family Collection.)

And now another story from the GU. Same horse, different kid. A young man wrote to me to tell me that one day when he was a small child, he was sitting on the horse waiting for his mom to load her groceries. A man walked by and put a quarter in the machine so he could have a ride. His mother told him that man was Oscar Brand. It wasn't until he was older that the name meant anything to him.

That is my father, kindness with no reward. And that is me. I learn everyone's name and where they're from, introduce myself to every business person or serviceman, offer water on a hot day to the mailman, etc.

I used to think I did this because I have been in sales my adult life, but now as I write, I realize how and when it all started, way back with my Dad and his kindness towards everyone. I have no musical talent whatsoever, but sales were a natural for me, always the leader and always remembering a name or anniversary. People love that; it makes them feel special and I just can't help myself. I want everyone to be happy and if I were truly honest, I want them to like me as well.

Chapter Four

Remembering Croton is like remembering a dream. The house is long since gone. Burned to the ground after we moved. A football field in its place. The people and the music also gone, mostly remembered in books and on recordings, their legacies written and sung about at tribute concerts. All that energy and possibilities of changing the world through music seem diminished somehow. But I think we were fooled by hope. After Croton, not much went right. But we're still there, as much in our memories as in the people who still remember us. So much happened in those incredible three years.

In second grade, while I made schoolgirl chums and worked out to "The Chicken Fat" song, the world was going through a crisis. The Cuban Missile Crisis. So a "fire drill" in school became an "air raid" drill. We were either instructed to hide under the desk, so the flying glass from the windows wouldn't hurt us, or to form a neat line in the hall, girls first, to go down a slide to the fallout shelter below. Girls first so the boys couldn't see up our dresses during a nuclear fallout. This impacted us in such subtle ways even to this day. I remember walking home from school and a plane might fly overhead. My first reaction was that I was about to have a bomb dropped on me. Over the years, I have talked to many children of this era. They all say the same thing.

What we didn't know at the time was that the true danger was indeed coming from the air, but not in the way of a bomb. Pesticides were dusting the heavily wooded areas upstate and we were rolling in the leaves. I stayed home for 10 days once when a mysterious rash appeared all over my arms and legs. Quarantined. No one figured out that I had been swinging from vines into leaf piles covered in DDT. It just wasn't part of the dialogue of the day. But as horrible as this sounds, and the future damage it may have done aside, this was a wonderful memory for me. Why? Because the night I came down with the high fever my father and mother both happened to be home. This was very unusual, as Dad was in the city most nights either rehearsing or performing, and my Mom might have been home, but we would not have known because she wasn't available.

I was quickly brought upstairs to the forbidden third floor and dumped into a bath of ice cubes. (This is not the good part.) But as my fever came down, I was wrapped in a towel and taken into bed with Mom and Dad. Cuddled between them for the first and only time I can remember. It was heaven and over by dawn.

Mother had an artist studio on the third floor and she decided that she should do a portrait of me after my close call. I truly hated sitting still as she painted. Her style was blue. Everything from landscapes to portraits were based in blue pigment. Not reminiscent of Picasso's "Blue Period," just the color base was always blue.

I still have that portrait, one of the only pieces I saved from Jean Ritchie's shed: where many years later my mother dumped the relics of our past life in exchange for money, I'm told. But I didn't know my mother by then and Jean was nice enough to let me have my portrait back. I'm not sure why it was important for me to have it. Now it seems very Gothic and fairytale like. I am sure the only reason she painted it because she thought I was going to die, or maybe not. I'm about eight in the portrait, but I look twenty and very sad.

No hands. My mother couldn't paint hands.

This is the perfect time to tell you about the gallery. Mother painted everyone who visited. Ralph Rinzler for instance, who had this marvelous angular face. I know she exhibited at the Washington Square Art Show every year. All those parties that lasted for days and all those famous people who ate and drank and sang into Dad's microphone were subjects for mother's paintbrush. Eventually the idea of opening a New York style art gallery in our one stoplight town, seemed to be a good idea.

The name was simply "The Village Gallery." Opening night was very exciting. The gallery sat on the main street, and the old Greenwich Village Crowd was invited along with our new friends from town. What I remember was earlier in the day peeling 300 frozen shrimp with the housekeeper for the big party that night. I also remember seeing a film once of the opening, but can't remember at whose house or where.

Portrait of Jeannie by her mother.
(Brand Family Collection.)

My mother, dressed in a little black dress with pearls, sported a *Jackie O* hairdo. She was slim and petite and totally in charge of the crowd. I do not remember seeing my father there, but maybe he was filming. A lot has been lost, but there remains a *New York Times* article about the gallery and how it's owner abandoned it after only two months. Now that seems about right.

Oblivious to the gallery closing, I did notice a lot of art covering our walls all of a sudden. Never thought about it. My mother busied herself with a herb garden and I was always at a friend's house after school. I was noticing that my father was not around that summer. I knew he traveled a lot for his work and festival hopping, but usually we went with him; this was different. Mostly, in the summer when Dad was home, we would go to Silver Lake and spend the afternoon with him. There was a shortcut through our property behind the school to get to the Lake and all the kids took it. We used to see them in the morning, but Dad didn't mind and never said a word. Mom had her B.B. gun by the back door, but that was for bears; so I guess she didn't mind or care either.

I remember asking the housekeeper where my father was after a few days of missing him. Her eyes had been glued to the television for days. She pointed to the little black and white TV and said, look closely at all those people arm in arm marching together and singing. There's your daddy. I had no idea what or why he was there; I only cared that he wasn't home. Now I know he was with Martin Luther King Jr. showing his solidarity and I am proud of that today. Then, I just wanted him to take me to the lake.

Years later, I was reading the obituary of Leon Bibb, the actor, singer, and civil rights activist, and there was a photograph of my father on stage with Bibb, Peter Yarrow, Mary Travers, Harry Belafonte, and Joan Baez all singing on the steps of the Montgomery, Alabama State House. It was the third historic march, and proved that my memory serves me well; but there is a back story that only family knows, and it sheds some light on the real dangers of those times.

During the rally performance Dad stepped off the stage for a moment to go look for a soda shop or gas station where he could answer nature's call. He'd no sooner taken a few steps when a large man blocked him and said, "Please get back to the stage, or I can't protect you." It was at that moment, he related to us later, that he realized the extent to which he, and all the others, were putting themselves on the line. This is a history lesson for me, but also a life lesson. Being on the side of right is rarely safe or easy. I'm sill proud in 2016 to be reading about this time and the chances people took to change the way we look at our fellow humans. Maybe especially in this time.

From left: Harry Belafonte, Leon Bibb, Joan Baez and Oscar Brand
performing in Selma.
(Photo Credit: Steve Somerstein.)

And then it happened. We all know where we were the day President Kennedy was killed. The young, handsome president, full of hope for our country. We were sent home from school to watch the mournful sight of a national tragedy unfold. I stood in the maid's quarters, watching her television because I felt most comfortable there. I didn't really understand, of course, what this meant; but with the adults so upset, I knew it wasn't good and there would be no big three day Thanksgiving party this year at the Brands'.

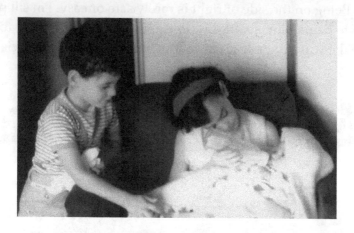

Jeannie feeding baby James, with Eric looking on, 1964.
(Brand Family Collection.)

That winter my mother took a little trip abroad. Didn't seem unusual as she hated the winter in Croton and everyone was used to one or another of my parents being absent. I didn't know at the time that she had left my father for another man, but I do know now that when she returned she and my father reunited. Nine months later my youngest brother was born. Of course, this is information I should not know and when I watched the old film of the trip to the hospital for my brother's birth, everything seems so unbalanced. A wave, a snapshot of the sign outside Tarrytown Hospital, and then a baby – not in my mother's arms, but in a nanny's.

My mother never went near my brother. The nanny's corner on the first floor had a nursery, bathroom, and private adjoining room. I visited often and loved and held my brother. Even changed him once or twice. But I never saw my mother with him, not even once.

In one more sweeping gesture of outrageous behavior, my mother adopted another dog and named him *Kelso*, after the man she had been having an affair with. Of course we never knew any of this. Big, stupid, friendly, Kelso. An Irish setter that would never be leashed and ran around the property, into the lakes and ponds, sprayed by skunks, and in general uncontrollable. And that is where the old 16mm film ends. Baby James playing with Kelso on the lawn. How ironic, and how twisted.

James with Kelso, Croton, 1964. (Brand Family Collection.)

Dad was at this point spending a great deal of time working on the musical "A Joyful Noise." I became good friends with the star's little girl during rehearsals, when school was out. She was a couple of years older and bored, so we put on our own plays and musicals. She was funny and talented even then.

This was John Raitt's daughter, Bonnie Raitt. Many years later, when Bonnie was trying to jump start her own career as a singer, she appeared at a church in the Village and invited my father to come to her concert. I think she was about eighteen at the time. I went along for the pure adventure of it and because I cherished a little alone time with my Dad.

She was as purely talented and exciting as she is to this day, only seeking out my father for his blessing and reassurance. I am so happy for her and the successful career she deserves. Watching her win a Grammy with her father in the audience is a very special memory for me, but mostly because I remember being there from the beginning and how proud her father, who has long ago passed away, looked in the audience that night.

Jeannie and James, Croton, 1965.
(Brand Family Collection.)

I thought about a time when my father might be as proud of me. I know as an adult, that his children all make him proud without question and for so many reasons. But every child seeks approval; it is part of their character. Without it, we can wind up searching for it in all the wrong places.

Words & Music by Oscar Brand and Paul Nassau, 1966.

I am positive now that my father kept a small apartment in the Village for overnight stays. How else could we have kept our old telephone number when we wound up back in the Village? I also seem to remember one or two overnights myself, but not clearly. When we weren't going to a festival or concert we were home based in Croton. I cannot explain why I decided to test my folks at eight years old, but I think I was beginning to catch on that our lives were not typical.

I decided to run away. I walked all the way into town, a considerable distance. I spent the day at the library and then walked home and hid in our garden shed.

No one missed me. Seriously, the babysitters thought I was

with my mother and the housekeeper thought the same. All I know is that my father came home and was furious – but not at me. I was not punished; actually the opposite, I was asked for forgiveness because no one had realized I was gone.

It was during the Croton period that I took horseback riding lessons. Private? No, that would really be unseemly, so the 4-H club it was. Every Wednesday after school in Croton, someone's mother drove, never mine, never Dad, but always someone we knew. We really learned everything there was to know. Spent most of the time grooming someone else's horse and shoveling manure. At the end of the two hours, we got to ride around in a circle for 20 minutes. Big payoff for all the work. I would like to say I loved it. I can't remember, but it may have been the reasoning behind why my brother and I were shipped off to a riding camp. Even though at 5, my brother had never even seen a horse except on television.

There was, however, an ulterior motive. Mother, who had at first insisted on a life in the country, now refused to spend another winter in Croton. She demanded a return to the city. I had just finished fourth grade. But I had no idea of all this when my brother and I were sent to camp that summer. Neither of us realized we would never see our friends, our pets, or the big house again. *Deja vu.*

Chapter Five

Unaware that the great move was taking place, my brother and I boarded the bus for camp. Lively and fun, I only remember noise and excitement, so I figured this was a good thing. I had already gotten used to watching out for my younger brother at the day camp we went to. It wasn't difficult. He was a timid, well behaved little guy. It wasn't until my younger brother, five years his junior, started messing with him that he became a wild, untamable, torturing, factor in my life. He really hates that now. If he ever reads this, it will make him very upset, because all grown up he became my protector and such a decent guy and family man. They both did. But we are nowhere near that future. We are on our way to camp. And quite literally, on our own.

The decisions of the adults in charge of this camp were – *how can I convey this?* – probably made under duress or under the influence of something. I have no other explanation for why I was put in a bunkhouse with older girls, to be teased unmercifully for the entire time I was there. I could have been assigned to a younger group, then I would have been the oldest. That would have made sense; but except for being called upon whenever there was a sleepless night for Eric, or a boo-boo that needed a big sister to help, I was on my own with the mean girls. Everyone there got CARE packages from home, but wouldn't share with me because I didn't get one.

Letters from home were a big deal; but there were none for us.

The first week was swim testing. I wasn't very good, having learned in a lake to doggie paddle to the nearest rock. So I was assigned to the beginner group. This was fine with me, except for the fact that I could ride horseback pretty well and the beginner swimmers were, you got it, beginners on the horses. So my time with the horses was mostly shoveling manure again! Advanced horsemanship took place while the beginners were swimming!

This pretty much sums up the entire 6 weeks of camp. It was miserable and lonely. Even the counselors started to notice and felt sorry for me. I always got picked for the team games first. Best nose thumbing I could think of!

One day during "color wars" I accidently stepped into a hive of bees. They swarmed around me and the counselor who was trying to help me out. We were both stung pretty badly. An ambulance took us to a local hospital, but no one was able to reach my parents. I was hysterical, afraid that I might never be going home at all. I mean who leaves their kids at camp *and moves?* My brother and I were somewhere in Pennsylvania, and *no one* knew where my parents were. That's the way I remember it. My father will say he was in Canada doing a T.V. show and of course there was a forwarding address and telephone number. OK, I believe him. Doesn't mean anyone answered.

On the last night before we boarded a bus for home, there was a dance. I went only because I was in the older girls' bunk. It was my first boy/girl experience. No one asked me to dance and by nine o'clock it was pretty obvious that no one was going to. Then the song "See You In September" came on and one of the cute counselors asked me to dance! Right in front of my bunkmates. It was awesome.

I was totally in love for 2.5 minutes, and then a big shot for the all-night discussion that followed. One brief moment of storytelling and rapture and I was hooked. Okay, that's what it takes. I could do that, I have and I'm doing it now. Are you aware that you're part of this excitement right now?

Well you are. And things are just warming up.

The next day, the final day of camp, the big "O" came and sang some folk songs and party songs for the whole camp. Everyone made a big fuss over us. They weren't aware that my father was famous. So what did that mean? We would have been treated better? Listened to with deference? I could have ridden in the horse show? Who knows, because by then it was a moot point. I pretty much had it figured out that Dad showing up alone and entertaining meant two things: camp was paid for and Mom was on holiday.

But this time I was wrong on that second point.

We were driven to our new townhouse in New York City, on West 11th Street in the Village. The drive was long and there was a lot of explanation of why the city was better for the family and Dad's career. He was working more and more on NBC children's programming and on Broadway. It made sense to us. We'd see him more often. But although that part is true, what we didn't anticipate was how we were going to see more of him if he lived on a different floor. And that's what happened.

The night we arrived "home" was like some tragic play. It was late and we were exhausted. As I followed my father, I was keenly aware that we bypassed the first two floors via outside stairs to get to the "children's apartment" on the third floor. There was no other way to reach the apartment downstairs except through the outside doors. Meanwhile, my parents enjoyed a beautiful duplex apartment with a winding staircase. The first floor of their apartment included a living room, a complete kitchen, and even an outdoor patio. The second provided a master bedroom and two studios. Here was privacy taken to a whole new level. Locked doors instead of rules. I got it immediately. It took my younger siblings longer.

All my cats had been adopted by others, or perhaps just left behind. I'll be kind and think they were OK. We met the nice nanny that would be living on our floor, taking care of my littlest brother. Of course, it felt reassuring to have an adult on our floor. We were told to be very quiet at all times because there was a tenant on the fourth floor. I never met her, although I sneaked up the stairs once just to see if it was true, and it was.

There was also a really creepy basement – stone walls carved out of the bedrock that lays beneath Manhattan. My mother used it for the fallout shelter storage where she stored canned goods and, of course, wine. We put on puppet shows and plays down there because it seemed forbidden and fun.

We didn't spend a lot of time at the brownstone during that late summer. The World's Fair had opened in New York. We made frequent visits there. It was always very exciting because our father had written the theme song for the fair, Dad doing the singing. I felt really special as if the world and the fair belonged to me.

Autumn arrived. I walked to school every morning. Here I was back once again at P.S. 41, but now in 5th grade, with no one familiar from 1st. Add to that a tough little schoolteacher.

I have been thinking recently, as I write, that maybe I am being a little unfair in my assessment of this bizarre family dynamic. I've asked myself the obvious questions about what a little girl needs to complete her development into a decent adult. Obviously, there are going to be glitches given the circumstances of the times and the already dysfunctional drama taking place, but I did have a couple of advantages, besides the nannies and housekeepers. For instance, I was given dance lessons. Not ballet lessons, like most little girls from the fifties, but dance lessons. I took them with Leish Clancy, Paddy's daughter. I was birdlike and gawky, she not so much.

I hated the lessons, but liked her. As I recall, she was giggly and awkward. So we hit it off right away and were immediately dismissed from class for talking too much and laughing. Just for fun, I looked Leish Clancy up on Facebook and she friended me right away. She says she remembers the giggling too. We actually live quite close to each other and are planning to meet up soon.

And now in New York there was also my first little boyfriend. A cutie pie with an ascot I kid you not. Fred would walk me home or meet me for a bike ride to Abington Square Park. The Village hadn't changed much in three years; only I had grown up enough to realize that kids my age were having challenges our parents never dreamed of. I met many children from single parent households. Two of them became my best friends. At first this seemed fascinating to me, just a mother in charge – a mother who *cared*. It was so foreign and yet desirable. The reality was how poor both these friends seemed to be, abandoned by their fathers. But at the time it seemed exotic and fun to live in one room with your mother and her cats. Not a lot of rules like at our house. Just a lot of independence which seemed very dangerous and cool.

We settled into the routine of homework, "Dark Shadows," the now-classic vampire soap opera, and dinner. Dad's T.V. career meant it was normal for us to have a television at the table while we were eating. We watched the "Monkees" and then "Laugh-In." My dad only griped at the smoking, never the politics or risqué jokes. Then off to bed.

A short time later I remember the dining table littered with paper scraps and receipts. Dad was being audited, a popular way for the government to harass Left-wing folksingers back then. This would go on for the next twelve years and was very stressful. Fortunately, he was a meticulous receipt keeper, and I learned this lesson myself very early on. I always keep receipts and pay my taxes on time.

Occasionally, more than I would have liked, my mother would take me to a tavern called *The Lion's Head*, a gathering place for folk musicians and artists. Dad was not in town on these occasions, or was otherwise engaged. I know he wouldn't have allowed it if he had known. Later when he did find out, he used this information to help him get custody. A rarity in those days. Not that my mother wanted custody (although she might well have taken me at one point), but a bargaining chip was a bargaining chip.

I haven't any idea why she brought me. A kid could go anywhere and no one blinked – but on a school night, with the drinking and singing and smoke and noise, it was weird. The good thing is that I heard people singing and enjoying themselves because they wanted to share and swap songs, my favorites always the Clancy Brothers, because they were so warm and were never mean drunks.

But I also saw Barbara and Logan English get drunk and they seemed to hate each other. I was ten; this wasn't fun.

At that moment I put together my life's motto: singing and fun were good; drinking, not so much. I slowly learned other important lessons. Saying *no* is an option. Not always, but at least there is the illusion of defiance. I always felt after that giant move from the country to the city with no warning, that anything could happen at any moment; and I was spot on right.

So many memories of that first year.

My father had a writing partner – Paul Nassau - and they were going to write what they believed would be the next big Broadway hit. I believe this time around it was "The Education of Hyman Kaplan." In those days, you invited some people with money to your house – they were the potential "Backers" – and then Dad and his partner Paul would tell the whole story of the show and sing the songs to the audience in the living room. If they agreed to foot the bill, the next step was producing the play. It was just like the movies that you see today, about the good old days, very much like Mel Brooks's "The Producers," which I love and reminds me of that time. Except without the larceny.

If my father was in town, and not booked for an early evening interview or performance, or otherwise engaged, he would come to us before we went to sleep and lay on my brother's bottom bunk bed, singing to us. He was so relaxed. I would come in from my room and lay with them. We'd all sing songs together, then I'd go to my room and fall asleep.

Those were good nights on West 11th Street. Dad made a lot of promises then, about the family trips we would be going on and adventures. He told marvelous stories, never scary, always funny. But remembering the songs he sang now, about drowning sailors, and Henry the Eighth disposing of Anne Boleyn, I wonder why we didn't have nightmares!

PREMIERE PERFORMANCE, APRIL 4, 1968
ALVIN THEATRE

ANDRÉ GOULSTON / JACK FARREN
AND STEPHEN MELLOW

present

TOM BOSLEY

in

THE EDUCATION OF

H*Y*M*A*N K*A*P*L*A*N

A New Musical

Book by **BENJAMIN BERNARD ZAVIN**
Music & Lyrics by **PAUL NASSAU & OSCAR BRAND**
Based Upon The Stories by **LEO ROSTEN**

with

BARBARA MINKUS

NATHANIEL FREY   **GARY KRAWFORD**

HONEY SANDERS ● DICK LATESSA ● BERYL TOWBIN

DAVID GOLD ● DONNA McKECHNIE ● DOROTHY EMMERSON and MIMI SLOAN

RUFUS SMITH • STEPHEN BOLSTER • WALLY ENGELHARDT

DICK ENSSLEN • DAVID ELLIN • SUSAN CAMBER

and **HAL LINDEN**

Settings Designed by **WILLIAM & JEAN ECKART**
Costumes by **WINN MORTON**   Lighting by **MARTIN ARONSTEIN**
Musical Direction and Vocal Arrangements by **JULIAN STEIN**
Orchestrations by **LARRY WILCOX**   Dance Music Arranged by **LEE HOLDRIDGE**
Production Stage Manager **EDWARD PRESTON**
Associate Producer **DAVID W. SAMPLINER**   Assistant to the Producers **VIVIAN FARREN**
Dances and Musical Numbers Staged by **JAIME ROGERS**

Production Directed by
GEORGE ABBOTT

Opening Night: April 4th 1968 – the night of Martin Luther King Jr.'s assassination. When word reached the theater, everyone – including the Mayor of New York City – departed during the first act. All of Broadway went dark, as did the show itself very shortly.

The family had many good friends in the neighborhood. Just down a block on Bank Street was Theodore Bikel. He was a very close friend of my father's. I too loved him and spent a summer babysitting for his two young boys. I understand that after his divorce, his sons did not speak with him again. This is so tragic, for I do know that he was beyond thrilled to be a father.

I remember a special Passover at Theo's house. To this day Dad plays a recording of that night on his radio broadcast because the singing was so memorable. But the tape only includes *some* of the wonderful singing, which lasted for about three hours. Theo also recited the entire original Passover story – beautifully. Finally, when we children had listened and squirmed and did our best to behave for the delicious reward to come, the Passover feast. The one thing we hadn't counted on: Theo's wife Rita was a terrible cook!

With all due respect, I am truly serious. Not an edible morsel. The radio broadcast is an intimate treasure belonging to the ages, but the meal was completely forgettable. Well, maybe not, since I remember it to this day.

Each one of my brothers has a special story we all tell differently from this time in our lives. My brother James, about two years old now, got the idea that if he tied a towel around his neck and opened the window he could fly like Superman! He was caught just in time, but we realized this kid had a real escape issue and maybe he should be under watch all the time. Good thinking. So he got a lot of attention. My brother Eric will swear to this day that he thought it would be funny to scare James by hiding behind a door at the top of the stairs and shouting "Boo!" Funny maybe to a seven year old – but I happened to see my two year old brother fly down the stairs and land badly on a Batman toy car. Luckily, St. Vincent Hospital was across the street. There and then Eric became, in my eyes, a devious monster. I didn't get the whole "negative attention is better than no attention" thing yet. I just wanted to stay under the radar. Many kids, when things go south, blame themselves. But in my case, I knew just where to place the blame.

It was a wild time in our house. I now know that my parents were seeing a marriage counselor who gave them the classic '60s advice of having an "open marriage." The reason for this bizarre new age recommendation was that because my mother never really experienced a childhood or dating, since she had been performing all her life through her adolescence and early adulthood, she felt she had missed out. Meanwhile, my father had already established himself as a typical alpha male, entertainment magnet, and terrific flirt. Despite his flirtations, Dad wanted to keep the family intact; and mother seemed to somehow need "permission" to do what they were both doing anyway. No condemnation here. That's just the way it was and clearly being exiled to one floor made it possible for us children to be completely unaware of the antics going on elsewhere in the house. Except of course for me, as I was older, had more understanding and also – sadly – more exposure.

One strange day, without so much as a thought as to how what was about to happen might affect me forever, my mother invited me to her bedroom upstairs. I had literally never seen it before. It was huge, overlooking the garden. Had a master bathroom too.

I had seen their studios, Dad's with his Omni unit and record collection, along with his recording devices; and Mother's crowded with art supplies she never used anymore. Going to Mom's bedroom was a whole new experience and I was so excited! I thought maybe I had been invited for "the talk."

But again – surprise, surprise – my visit lasted only for the two minutes it took for me to be instructed to open the double closet doors, where I found a very naked, very embarrassed, beautiful blond girl hiding: Do you see that?" my mother asked. Then she dismissed me. This moment changed me, and has stayed with me. I think it must have been a turning point of some sort for my parents as well.

Much later, when I confronted my father about this bizarre day, he said that he'd thought my mother was out and had given his friend access to the apartment to take a shower. It didn't seem like such a big deal to him. It doesn't seem right though, no matter what their arrangement. But what I didn't know at the time was that my mother wasn't even actually living there anymore.

The "Family."
(Photograph by George Pickow.)

Chapter Six

It was the summer of 1967. We had lived in the town house for just under three years. Fifth grade is a blur; all I remember is taking violin lessons and playing second violin in the little makeshift orchestra. I had a new blue dress for the occasion of my graduation into Middle School, and a promise that my Dad would be there. He has few regrets in his life, but I know that his missing this day is one of them. He swears he sent beautiful roses to me for this milestone; but I never got them. The emphasis being on the flowers not being delivered and not the occasion. It seems to matter more to him than to me.

I never expected either one of my parents to come for anything except maybe a school concert that Dad was giving. That was guaranteed. In fact, later in my life, all grown up and married, but living far away, I would arrange publicity and gigs for Dad in my neighborhood for the express purpose of having him visit. Truly an entertainer's daughter, understanding that he would come if it involved a performance. That's not a criticism, just our way of life. But that summer was really important to us. Our entire family dynamic changed and I had my first real crush.

My father rented a cottage by the water in Hampton Bays, Long Island for my mother, so that she could "rest." We still went to the Festivals, but I distinctly remember that my mother did not go with us. Actually, I have no memories of her *ever* having gone with us.

This year, during the Newport Festival, we stayed at a motel which boasted a pool. Very, very cool and much fun for kids. A young, skinny, long haired guy splashed around in the pool with my brother and me. He noticed I couldn't swim properly and offered to teach me. He had this mellifluous voice and was so nice though obviously a teenager, which made it even more exciting to me. Well, as he would say almost 50 years later to me, "I guess I did a good job; you didn't drown." That nice young man was Arlo Guthrie. I didn't know him then except as Woody's son. And that day at the pool, I didn't know that it was a day before he would become a household name.

The next morning, Arlo was working out a song at a workshop session. My father heard him singing and asked him about it. Arlo said he had spent about two years on that song and he was almost ready. My father wisely told him it was time, and put him on the main stage at Newport that night, where he performed "Alice's Restaurant" for the first time before a live audience. The audience went crazy. Arlo never thought a song that long would ever get radio play or a record, but that's just history now.

For my Father's 95th birthday, Arlo recorded a video message that basically thanked Dad for giving him his career. Earlier on that broadcast, Dad recalled that in 1967 he'd moved his annual Cooper

Union Festival to Carnegie Hall, while Cooper Union underwent renovation. The guests included Pete Seeger, Judy Collins, Jean Ritchie and young Arlo in his first major post-Newport appearance. Mayor John Lindsay gave an opening address, and Arlo performed "Alice's Restaurant" to an enthusiastic reception.

I've heard lots of stories over the years about Arlo's "folk" Bar Mitzvah and Dad's involvement in his life, but by far the 95th birthday video says it all. Arlo is the consumate performer in every sense: witty and talented, with a folk pedigree that cannot be matched. He's proved himself all these years while still remaining as approachable and nice as that young man who taught me to swim. My first crush.

Sometime during the second half of that summer we were dropped off at my mother's place in the Hamptons.

"We" did not include my youngest brother, James. While my father was there, yes, James was with us. We fished off the dock while Mom slept late, and seemed like the typical family on vacation. But only one day after arriving, my father left me and my brother Eric at the beach and drove back to Manhattan with James. I understood immediately and became quietly enraged. I could handle my brother Eric on my own: entertain him and feed him while mother slept in and around. But leaving little James there would be "inconvenient" for her.

That summer was a turning point. My brother woke me in the middle of the night to tell me that Mother was crying out and was hurt. I jumped out of bed and dashed to her door where I did indeed hear crying, but it wasn't from pain and she wasn't alone. I took Eric outside the house in the dark by the edge of the water, lit only in moonlight, and explained that everything was fine, and I would always be there to take care of him. The next day we called my father to come get us. Thank goodness he was in town and he did.

By then it was obvious that the marriage was over. My mother had fallen in love. Always a danger I guess when given permission to date while married. The "object of her affection" – I know it's cliché, but it's all I have at the moment – was a nice fighter pilot whose parents owned the cottage we had rented. He was scheduled to go to Vietnam that fall.

I guess perhaps he seemed heroic and stable and the complete opposite of my father, which really isn't fair because there is no one more heroic and stable than my father. Tragically, he was killed in action. But by that time decisions had already been made and another great move was underway.

All we children were aware of was that our upstairs apartment was under construction. Actually the only room that was physically changed was mine. It was being made into a kitchen, so the new buyers would have another apartment to rent. I wasn't consulted or even part of the packing up and moving of my things. I just hung out in my brother's room while the workmen hacked and banged, and slept on a cot at night. I do not remember feeling any anxiety at all. I figured that this was a good idea to have our own kitchen upstairs. I never suspected I would be displaced. I trusted yet again, that I would be taken care of. But of course, this was a mistake.

Chapter Seven

Autumn 1967: My new school proved to be a little bit of a challenge. First of all, it was located in the Chelsea neighborhood of the city, which at the time was mostly Hispanic. So, being a bright little thing, I chose to take Spanish lessons, which truly came in handy. Still does.

I fell back in with my two best friends from elementary school, Dana and Diana, and some other kids in our grade. There was one young man who boasted the name *Jacque Guillotine;* and yes his family could trace their roots to that famous ancestor, the sinister inventor! So, good for me, another person who had the limelight; I liked that and we became friends.

The only time I felt any threat at all was the first few days of gym. It wasn't the kind of physical threat you might expect. It was more cultural. I was still wearing an undershirt and most of my Hispanic classmates were in bras. Some were hiding baby bumps already, and I was completely naïve about this. This embarrassment was offset by my abilities in gymnastics. I was excellent in all sports, being tiny and thin. I know this will surprise anyone who knows me now, as puberty hit me like a tornado, completely ravaging me. But before that I won the President's Fitness Award and was darn proud. The worst day was that of the cafeteria prank: pulling my zippered dress down with taunts about my undershirt. My nickname became "Jeannie Stringbeanie," and it stuck.

The second challenge of the school was its location. I had to either take a bus or subway to school each morning alone. The subway was better, but I've always been sensitive to noise, so more often I chose the bus. Only problem was that I had to walk past the meat packing district on 8th Avenue which was pretty horrific and not a great way to start or end a school day.

I was completely stunned when by November and the first snowfall, I realized I had only been treading water all this time, waiting for the vortex to pull me under.

It was a freezing night, with snow already covering the ground and still falling. I looked out my bedroom window, now just a kitchen with plastic sheets everywhere and my cot. I don't know why at that moment I decided to look. Maybe I heard yelling and a slamming door. That would have been unusual; so I looked. I saw my mother in her bright red rabbit fur coat walking out. I was dressed only in my nightgown but I went tearing out into the snow barefoot. I ran after her pulling on her coat, while she screamed at me to get back inside.

Now possibly this might have been the worst night of her life. I wasn't aware of that, but I certainly know it felt like mine. I knew if I let go of that coat that would be it. I felt so responsible to keep her at home with us, so that nothing would change. But she actually peeled my hands from her and kept walking. I couldn't believe it. I had no choice but to return to the house, and to bed.

It never occurred to me to knock on the second floor door and talk to my father. I just assumed it was over. I was helpless and since he was still here, we'd be okay.

I went to school the next day, and in the afternoon, to my surprise, both my father and mother were home waiting to take me to the movies. The movies! How absolutely absurd. Neither of them ever took us to the movies and certainly never together. I knew instinctively what was coming but I wanted this time for me alone, so we went. We saw a movie called *After the Fox* with Peter Sellers, at the Waverly Theatre.

Probably some therapist had told them to take their oldest child to a nice neutral place before her family imploded. I can't think of another reason, because after the drama the night before, it was pretty much a forgone conclusion. This was the end.

Dad explained that they were divorcing and that the town-house had already been sold. My mother had actually moved out that summer into a nice apartment by Sheridan Square. To put things more bluntly: my father, my two brothers and I wound up in a third story walk up, and my mother had a fabulous penthouse all to herself as well as a summer house in the Hamptons.

Our new Perry Street apartment was tiny. Dad quickly tried to give all of us some privacy and to set up some rules. First of all, he took the giant closet with a window as his room – quickly filling it with his bed and his records and his Omni unit. Meanwhile, he divided the one and only big room with a curtain so that my brothers had a tinge of privacy. Of course a curtain isn't much privacy for mischievous boys, but that was at least the thought behind the curtains.

Then knowing a girl needed even more privacy, Dad had a sheetrock wall put up dividing what should have been a dining room, right outside the kitchen. He allowed enough room for a bed, chest of drawers and in an enlightened moment, a giant mirror on the back of the door for the illusion of space.

The living room had an oddly colored yellow couch, which turned out to be a convertible, as if guests were an option. But Dad always thought when he bought a couch that it should be a convertible. He had had so many experiences putting people up all those years that it was ingrained in his make-up. And indeed, he later started doing it again. We also had one arm chair and a table which literally unfolded like Saran Wrap. Two handles that you pulled, and out came a table for six. Like a Murphy bed, but for dinner. Later I learned that it had been a gift from Dick, my godfather, since my mother had taken all the antiques.

I cannot even begin to think how Dad must have felt about these arrangements. He never let on about his feelings. We were just kids anyway. But immediately, a predictable new life emerged that would place me in the awkward, and not very happy, position of substitute caregiver.

Every morning, a bicycle at the ready, we would head off to school. James in the booster seat on back, Dad riding, and Eric walking off to elementary school right around the corner. I would walk as far as 14ᵗʰ Street, Dad and James riding by my side, and say goodbye. James would then be dropped at the Sisters of Nazareth, a pre-school on 12ᵗʰ Street. The benefit to having a Dad who worked nights, I guess. At least we had some supervision in the morning. After school, I would pick up James, and Eric would come home on his own.

There were two meals served at Perry Street. *Familia*, in the morning, invented by my father and not what you are thinking of at all, but his version. Grapenuts dumped into a giant aluminum pot mixed with raisins and nuts. Not bad, but not every day!

The evening meal was often his specialty: spaghetti with B&B mushrooms and Hunt's Tomato Paste out of the can. Not sauce mind you, paste. The great thing about all of this to Dad was that it could be reheated for three nights, feed all of us, and he had bragging rights to his cooking abilities! By Friday the special "Slab 'O Beef" came out. London Broil made on one of those broilers for the top of the stove. This was a huge treat for everyone but me. I could never stomach it and still tease him about it to this day.

I had no idea at the tremendous loss he took to eventually gain custody of all three of us: my mother's life of luxury was the price he paid. I didn't know that my mother would have gladly taken just me by that time; I was older and could take care of myself, and her. But my father believed in keeping the family together no matter what; this proved a good move, since losing her lover turned her into a tortured drunk with a lithium habit. I had no knowledge of any of this. I only knew that I was suddenly poor and feeling claustrophobic in that tiny apartment.

So now I became one of "those" girls. We were the three musketeers: Dana, Diana and I. Children of divorce, not much supervision; and two with the odd desire to see at least one of their mothers marry my father, so we could all be happy again. Funny what little teenybopper girls dream of. This seemed like a really good solution to all our problems. Little did we know then that this was just the beginning and only two of us would survive until our sixteenth birthday.

Mid sixties.

Chapter Eight

By the time everyone had settled into a routine, it became clear that there would be too many nights that my father would be out and this might not be a good idea, not only for me and the little rascals my brothers had become, but also as potential leverage for my mother in divorce court. Actually, my mother never even tried to get custody, but still the risk loomed large in my father's mind and effected him greatly. No one knew better than him how eratic and whimsical she could be. He'd not relax until divorce papers were finalized, and his custody locked in for good.

So he had an idea to offer the tiny space outside the kitchen to an NYU student in need of a place to stay, in exchange for babysitting duties. Good plan, except for the fact that it literally changed nothing for me. She was only there late at night, and she was a pre-med student with an affinity for showing us really disgusting photos from her collection of pre-med books. My first foray into sexual education, it was beyond description. Actually, when I needed a *real* question answered, I went to my friend's mother. Being a hippie, single mom in the 1960's, I fugured she would have all the answers.

One night, I was sleeping over at my best friend Diana's house. Her cat had just given birth to five kittens on my bed – right between my legs, on a blanket. Somehow this seemed like the perfect opportunity to approach the whole sex talk business with Diana's mother. Her answer was to give us a copy of "SCREW" Magazine. While we perused the photos and she cleaned up from the kitten birth, she asked us if we had any questions and we shook our heads *no*. I think we were in shock. Then she took away the magazine and that was that.

It was very disturbing and neither of us ever spoke about it. I still had very real questions and no one to ask. So, back to Perry

Street, with a couple of forays to mother's apartment thrown in, just to see how the other half lived.

Eric, James, and Jeannie with their Dad at Newport, 1968.
(Brand Family Collection.)

It was quickly approaching the summer of 1968. Dad had a couple of important summer jobs. One of course, was Newport, the other was out of the country. A three week engagement in Charlottetown, Prince Edward Island. This trip might have been excruciating because of the three eight hours a day car rides, but it truly wasn't.

It was a grand adventure. Dad was smart enough to stop frequently and sleep at little motels with a pool each night. We sang songs and collected souvenirs. When we got to New Brunswick, we even outran a tornado, which we could see in the rearview mirror!

Every single one of us was sea sick on the Blue Nose Ferry to Prince Edward Island from the port in Nova Scotia – *not* a smooth crossing. My father had a habit of eating pistachio nuts and spitting the shells into the surf. It was so rough that they literally came back to haunt us! He took his motion sickness in stride, so we wouldn't worry. He would just get sick, smile, and say "Your turn." And we took it. Makes for a hilarious story later, but it obviously didn't seem too hilarious at the time.

The best part about that summer was the house he rented right on the water. As the tide went out each morning, we gathered mussels, which I boiled and Dad and my brothers devoured. I thought they were kind of sad, being left behind by mere chance. I ate bread. It was enough.

There were a couple of bicycles, and plenty of playing in the surf to do by day. I had some help from Dad then, so I had a little alone time on the bike. This was a great time to explore. The land was open and no one was around for miles. So naturally this brings us to the nighttime.

Being such a big star in Canada, selling out three weeks in one of that country's largest venues wasn't a big deal to Dad. But all I can remember is one detail: We had to go with him every night. He couldn't leave us alone at the cabin, too remote; so he took us. BUT he was singing his famous *Bawdy Songs*, and the management assumed children would not be a welcome presence in the audience. So the answer was to leave us outside the entertainment hall in the convention center until the concert was over. We could have the whole run of the place. Fantastic, just what I needed: a babysitting gig with two maniacs who could run and hide for a couple of hours while Dad performed. I know he had no choice, and the funny thing is that the concert was piped in on speakers, so we heard every word. Just exhausting to even think about, but by the time each concert was over, my brothers were safe and I had done my job.

I always had excellent communication with my father. Once, I complained bitterly that the boys were getting harder and harder to control and they didn't listen to me. But my father's answer was that his role was both father and mother, and he refused to come home and be a disciplinarian as well. So I lost all my power of the typical family declaration, "I'm going to tell Dad." My brothers knew the score. This just made them laugh and test the boundaries even more.

Most weekends during the school year my father had performance engagements to which he brought us along.

Even before this trip to Canada, my father had had a few gigs at the Playboy Club in New Jersey. I really liked the bunnies and everyone was very nice to me. It was kind of special back then to be around all these pretty ladies. The club was beautiful and exotic, unlike anything I had ever experienced. Believing that this was great fun for me and the fact that I didn't complain, I think my father actually believed it was okay to bring us along wherever he went. I had no idea that he really didn't have a choice as the student babysitter went home on weekends. I was already a veteran of the "Bring your child to a night club" experience. Although, of course an entirely different experience from my mother's midnight runs to drink and party at the Lion's Head or Limelight.

On some weekday evenings, he taught a course at the Bayonne Community Center. So we would play in the gymnasium while he was in class, and then we would go to a wonderful fan's house for dinner. So many stories from children of folksinger's were exactly like this. I am listening to Arlo Guthrie telling a story just like it on his CD about his famous father. The people that come and go, and especially the ones that helped out. Let's just call this story: "The Folksinger's Guide to Medical Care."

One of Dad's biggest fans was a physician who lived in Bayonne. I remember specifically stopping off at his closed office and getting my up to date immunizations after a performance. Then away we went to his house for dinner. Now that's a fan! But for me it was emotionally embarrassing to sit at the table directly across from a man who had just punctured my tush with a needle!

There was also another doctor on 14th street that we were free to go to whenever the need for personal care was involved. He was an older gentleman who would take a ten dollar bill from you, put it in his desk drawer, and then examine and write a prescription if necessary. No nurse, no receptionist, but a waiting room full of patients without health insurance.

I had started wearing braces for my tiny little jaw that was overcrowded. I would have been better off had they pulled a few to make room, but I think they (wrongly) saw a cash cow in my father, so I had railroad tracks. By the time my parents were divorced, I was just wearing a retainer, or shall I say not wearing it. A very minor transgression that Dad never noticed, and I felt free of all the horrible pain. The problem was I never visited the dentist to remove the steel bands around my molars. Just ignored the whole situation. Why bring it up if it would cause pain? I'll tell you why. Because I got into a nasty habit of stopping for candy on the way home from school. I think I was always hungry and this satiated me for a while. I had no idea that I would eventually lose my molars and eight teeth. This is particularly ironic because dad was doing commercials for *Crest* where a little girl comes running in saying: "Daddy, Daddy, I have no cavities!"

It was at about this time that I began to think of myself as overly burdened, and started to seriously fantasize – and that's the word, *fantasize* – that maybe the Sheridan Square penthouse, not to mention the Hamptons, might be more enjoyable. Not only creature comforts, but also an escape from Babysitter Land! Despite previous experience, I did not understand how dangerous this alternative actually was.

So one day I became the "grocery cart child." I have been trying to think of a suitable name for this crazy time in my life, and that's the best I can come up with because for about two days I played the *walk out* game. It was about the biggest mistake I could have made. My father knew it, but he had no power to stop me, as he explained later. Divorce proceedings were still pending, and any complaints might have cost him custody. He did not want to rock the boat with my unpredictable mother. So I packed up my grocery cart of a life (didn't have very much) and marched down Greenwich Avenue to Sheridan Square to my new life, unburdened of all that responsibility, or so I thought.

I guess most children of divorce at one time or another think the other parent might be a better fit. But in this case I was trading a good dad with a cramped apartment for a crazy psycho mother with a great view.

Chapter Nine

My first night at my mother's apartment was like a dream come true. Wow! A doorman and a beautiful living room decorated with all the art that I missed from Croton. A panoramic view of Manhattan's West Village topped off with the furniture from the big house. A very memorable velvet set of red chairs and a blue velvet couch.

My mother had a giant bedroom down the hall and I had a bed in an adjoining room to the kitchen, which she would later wall off and rent to a woman with 5 cats.

But that night it was all mine. I woke up to make myself breakfast and checked out the bathroom. A weird looking disk sat atop the commode. I opened it, and saw something I probably shouldn't have, but just kept in mind that I'd ask about it later when I asked my mother all the questions that had been building up anyway. The kind you can only ask your mother.

Yes, this was very nice. The subway was right downstairs. I felt no guilt for leaving what I deemed an impossible situation. I just needed to relax and form a relationship again with my mom. I did notice a painting on the wall, originally of my brother Eric and me, which had been painted over and now portrayed Eric and Kelso the dog. So maybe I really had done something to make her mad. I waited for her to wake up and offered to make breakfast.

The most unusual thing happened next. Mother had a few things to say about my moving in. First of all, I was to do all the housework; rent was high and she couldn't afford a maid. Second, I was to pay for my sheets because that was an added expense, but I could work it off by cleaning the fish tank and doing laundry. This was starting to smell like a set up.

But I went along, I did most of that stuff anyway at Perry Street and now I didn't have the beasts to care for, so it seemed feasible.

But that second night changed things forever.

First it was off to the Lion's Head for a few drinks. Mother met a young man, I believe younger than she was, and they got drunk together. So naturally she invited him back to the apartment to continue the party. I was sitting on the blue velvet sofa, not realizing what would come next.

Mother sat in the red chair laughing as the young man grabbed me, pushed me down, got on top of me, and rammed his tongue in my mouth.

They both thought this hysterically funny. He was grinding against me and I was squirming to escape; and I distinctly heard my mother laughing and saying something about having to learn sometime about the birds and the bees. Thankfully, this got a little boring for him, since he knew he was about to get laid for real. So off they went to her bedroom, and I packed up my shopping cart and headed for the elevator.

I walked into the Perry Street apartment late. Not a word was said or a question asked. I never told my father until it happened again years later, under very different circumstances. But I'm sure his reaction would have been the same: "You are a pretty girl. This will probably happen a lot. So take control. It's not your fault."

I hadn't even missed a day of school, but I had had quite an education. I never told anyone, and odd as this seems now, I still felt that when things got too difficult with my brothers, I had another option. I hope that doesn't sound strange, after such a traumatic experience. I would decide to test those boundaries again. It would be a very big mistake.

I am absolutely sure that my father hadn't any idea what was happening on a daily basis in his own home. He was always whistling, which I now know is a nervous tic, but I thought he was just a happy fellow. He was always concerned about his health, so even though his leg was quite an impediment, he took up roller-skating and swimming – making us go with him to the Leroy Street pool for workouts after school. As I recall, about as disgusting a place as you can imagine. All my childhood Village friends agree, but of course that was before the codes and renovations and the gentrification to the upscale place it pretends to be now.

I just made sure of course that everyone survived, and frankly I felt like I had added another child to my roster, my father, because we depended on him for everything, so he couldn't be hurt or challenged in any way. Therefore, I looked out for him too. Always the little mother. I even started calling him by his first name instead of *Dad*, which my friends found hilarious.

We were going to school and basically entertaining anybody we felt like bringing home. My friend Dana spent so much time sleeping over at my apartment, that her mother once half-jokingly threatened my father with kidnapping. At the same time, Dana and I got into the habit of cutting school and travelling around the city by ourselves, just because we could get away with it and it was fun. The Empire State Building was a favorite hang-out.

One day we actually were getting out of the subway, and my father was coming down the stairs right in front of us. We decided this city was smaller than we thought and maybe we should stick to a safer plan. So after everyone was delivered to school in the morning, we came back to the apartment, to watch daytime T.V. or gossip. Sometimes Dad would come home in the middle of the day and we would hide in my room under the mattress, giggling. Many years later, my father told me he knew we were there, and I asked him why he didn't say anything. He told me if I decided to cut school, I must have had a very good reason. No reprimand; that was it. And a very effective way of making me rethink skipping school, because he trusted me to make good decisions.

By then the good part of being twelve had kicked in. The nice boys and girls from our group at school had started having weekend parties. This was every week, and just a matter of whose house was available. Our apartment nearly always was, but it came with the two beasts. Dana's and Diana's places were too small. But there was always someplace to go and big excitement at the prospect of the new boy/girl aspect. I specifically remember asking my father for an allowance, so I could buy a new outfit for my first party. I had my eye on one of the handsome guys at school and I wanted this to be really special. We had exchanged at least a few shy looks and although we hadn't a clue about what happened at a party, I knew at least a new blouse would help my confidence. Dad obviously didn't have a clue either, because the answer was that I already had a blouse. Men just don't get it.

So, a little James Taylor on the record player and then we basically just hung out with the guys playing *Risk*, and trying to act cool. Pet the cat, flirt. I was out of my comfort zone, but luckily so was the object of my affection. We were just so young and mimicking the other kids who seemed to know a lot more than we did. I needed to learn fast. I really liked this guy. During one of the few parties at my apartment, one of the more knowledgeable guys suggested a game of Spin the Bottle. So now I got my first real kiss.

I have absolutely no memory of where this next party took place, but I do remember that this time my first, "boyfriend" was there. Everyone paired up for the classic, "Seven Minutes in Heaven." I remember this because we walked into the closet together and started to laugh. Neither one of us knew how to make the first move. He was so shy and even though I knew what to do, it wasn't my place. So we actually discussed how stupid the game was, and when seven minutes was up, we emerged a couple. Just taken for granted that now we were dating. Whatever that means at twelve, in the sixties. Just a smile or a glance in the hall. Not much more. But to our credit, this flirtation lasted all of intermediate school and we did date for real, on and off, beyond college. You never really forget your first love. Unfortunately, a good smack on the head later in my life and I did.

The one memory I do have – and since I recently reunited with the friend who threw this party, I can confirm its accuracy – was the night we all took a train to Brooklyn, where a friend lived, for a viewing of the movie "The Birds." This was a very special evening because everyone brought sleeping bags and we were going to spend the night. Boys and girls together. I think we were thirteen by then, and it was so exciting!

At about eleven o'clock I called the apartment just to be certain this was OK with my father. I was being courteous, as I distinctly remember asking in advance and receiving permission. So I was stunned to hear a very curt: "Come home immediately!" I tried to argue and was cut off: Now!" OK, so extremely disappointed and embarrassed at being the only one who had to leave, my date walked me to the subway and let me take a train home by myself.

What a guy, a girl alone on the subway at midnight.

I made it home safely, and walked into the apartment mad as hell at my father. He was in no mood. He explained how a sleep-over could jeopardize custody. I asked him why he didn't just explain that to me in the first place. His answer was that it was just easier to order me home. Maybe he was having a rough night too; I'll never know because I never asked. I felt awful and embarrassed, pretty upset too. So it was just about that time when I decided that keeping secrets was easier on everyone and since I was responsible for everyone's happiness, I would just keep everything to myself from then on. Big, big mistake – but impossible to do over. The shopping cart loomed large; I was angry and ready to pack up again.

Chapter Ten

I started spending much more time at my girlfriends' apartments. It was a good way to escape. Their mothers were so interesting and exotic. Dana's mother was one of the founders of NOW, The National Organization for Woman. She was always telling us horrible stories about men, and how even though she had passed Dana's father on the street in the Village, she would never tell Dana who he was. She changed her name and became a radical feminist. This left a permanent scar on my friend's heart and she tried so hard to make her tiny room into a little getaway, painted lively yellow, instead of the olive green her mother chose for the rest of the apartment.

Diana's mother was just weird – a verified hippie. Anything goes. Diana would go to her father's apartment often, looking for what was missing in her life, but he had started another family and she didn't fit in. We were just all misfits.

My father was dating again. I really shouldn't have been aware of this. But then a reporter calls your house when you are babysitting and says "Did you know your father is out with Carly Simon tonight?" My answer: "I only know he's out."

In those days, that was confirmation enough. When pressed, Dad would only say that his manager had set him up for publicity reasons. OK, I'll buy that at thirteen, but a big change took place.

My father hired someone full-time to live with us. He was performing more and more out of town. He rarely stayed away overnight, and actually gave up a European tour to be with us, but he realized that he needed an adult fulltime.

The person he chose to live with us in this tiny cramped place was a Miss Annie Sweeney. Full on Irish accent with a drinking habit very loosely disguised. I'm sorry, but I just cannot fathom how he didn't see this. Yes, she was fat, adorable, didn't mind having a bed with a curtain dividing her from her little charges. A joy to listen to. But the beer cans piled up under her bed to the point of being comical. And the smell! I will never be able to forget the smell of Annie. Just in time she met a big fireman and fell in love. We were the only ones to attend the wedding. My father gave her away.

But during this strange year of Annie, I decided this would be a great opportunity to spend some time over at the "House of the Rising Sun," my euphuism for my mother's apartment. I just needed a break.

Dad was never home on the weekends, he was performing more and more in clubs. Even the trips to GG's had stopped. And I didn't know at the time, but Dad was flirting with the possibility of a serious romance.

So off to Mother's I went, this time bringing Dana as backup. But even though we were welcomed, we had no place to sleep. By now my mother had built a wall next to the kitchen and rented space to the woman with five cats to make ends meet. I know she got alimony, but she was hedging her bets. Plus she had sublet the house in the Hamptons and the kids that signed the lease brought friends, lots of them. They had trashed the house and she was now involved in a contentious lawsuit. She was an unhappy person, drinking heavily and making embarrassing demands on the friends that she and my father once shared. No longer welcome at the Village bars because of her behavior and the fact that my father was well known and well liked, she drank at home.

I know she asked for money from these friends, and she sold a lot of her very valuable antiques and jewelry. That is how some of the treasures I recovered wound up with Jean Ritchie in her house. Each person she contacted heard terrible stories about my father, and some let her into their lives; it was a mistake. By the time they got wise, they either lost money or at the very least friendship with my father. Loyalty is everything to him. It is to me as well, probably where I get it from. But at least Jean and George stayed loyal and helped to return many things. I once saw an etching on their wall and remarked that my mother had done it. Jean said if you want it, just take it; so I did.

Dana and I quickly realized this was a sinking ship after a very brief time trying to make a normal life out of this crazy situation. Even when holding a Passover Seder which we cooked ourselves, Mom just drank the wine and then went off to bed. It wasn't going to work out; we never had a chance. I moved back to Perry Street and that September my mother moved to a small apartment on Bleeker Street with an ex-con that she had met. I guess they were in love. He played incredible piano and I was impressed enough after one visit to consent to spend the night; he was a nice guy and he really tried to control my mother's drinking. It only took that one night for her to decide that I was a threat at thirteen years old and send me packing at 2 AM. I actually walked home alone. It wasn't very far and the Village was always lit up and active at any hour, so I felt strangely safe, although completely humiliated.

I am reflecting now on why I was allowed such freedom at such an early age. Was it the necessity of growing up fast and being so responsible? Or was it just the fact that I was always available when needed, so no need for rules. I literally made my own decisions and was relied on heavily to step up when needed.

In 1968, so much was going on in the country. The unfathomable slaughters of Martin Luther King Jr. and Robert F. Kennedy. And the Vietnam War raging every night on television.

Convention riots, first in Miami and then in Chicago. Real police in riot gear against the citizens they were sworn to protect. Sound familiar? Dad was a liberal who spoke out and protested. He had campaigned for Humphrey, not that he believed that he was the best man for the job, but he was a Democrat and this time around, the third party alternative was George Wallace, the segregationist, who was actually making significant gains in the South. This landed dad on Nixon's "enemy" list. With our phone tapped and audits every year, this was turning into a nightmare.

Now my father was a target and so was the folk music community at large.

Dad performed at Café Lena in Saratoga Springs and the audience loved him. Funny stories were just what they needed during these turbulent times. Dad told jokes and knew the history behind the songs. He didn't just sing, he taught. As a matter of fact, he had a class at the New School before it was an accredited university. He would bring in Broadway friends and surprise the students with real stars, recalling their careers.

Dad was the Einstein of origins of songs, and loved educating the audience. My favorite story is about the song, "Kisses Sweeter that Wine." Did you know that originally this song was a Gaelic ode to a dead cow? The farmer only had one cow and when the cow died; he was bereft. This old song, with syncopation added by the great Leadbelly and new verses by the Weavers, became a hit for that group.

1968 was the year that Dad's musical "How to Steal an Election" debuted. It was and still is a masterpiece. This time it was off Broadway and a very young Clifton Davis and Carole Demos were the stars. I went to many rehearsals and I knew this was a very special show. All about politics, obviously; it's unfortunate for our country that it holds up today. The play revolved around the very courageous questioning of what we really deliver as a nation. So many songs were so important and right on in that show. Even as a young girl, I got the message. Sometimes in an election year he plays the soundtrack on his radio show. It was genius. I remember going to the opening, my first. It was so thrilling and full of passion and excitement. Just imagine the black star, Clifton Davis, belting out a song which questioned the liberals: "Comfort Me with Apples" (*Because I am sick of love. Love is lovely. I need something more.*) Very powerful for the time.

Also, the amazing anthem, "He's the Right Man." This song is sung twice. Once as a campaign fundraiser, with all the fanfare and dazzle, and later as a lament, alone by the female lead, under one spotlight, and slowly, almost as a love song. It stays with you long after the show is over. The show got excellent reviews and even a cast album. Many people believe it was written with George McGovern in mind. I know my father was a huge supporter, but I will never know for sure.

Music and Lyrics by Oscar Brand, 1968.

The ridiculous carnival atmosphere of the election process seemed like a caricature painting of what our democracy had become. The only good that emerged was the brilliance of the star, then an unknown Clifton Davis. About forty years later my father was tapped by the Smithsonian Institution to record an album of election songs going all the way back to George Washington. It became one of the biggest sellers of all time for their label, and earned my father a place on the "Daily Show" with Jon Stewart, which was cool for his teenage grandson.

The Smithsonian's annual Folklife Festival often included my father. Recently, I got a private tour, behind the scenes for the renovation of the Smithsonian Castle, plus lunch in the employee cafeteria. It was all very exciting to hear about the celebrities that required private access, like Tom Cruise and his entourage. It never occurred to me before to wonder how a celebrity and his/her family might make a trip to a museum without being mobbed by fans. But of course, Dad was never that famous.

Even before I was married and living in Washington, D.C., my father had a weekly radio program in addition to the WNYC show called "Voices in the Wind" on NPR. This required a weekly trip to Washington. This little gem of a broadcast contained many interesting interviews, including one with Justice William O. Douglas who laughingly admitted writing the bawdy lyrics to "Humoresque" while still in law school. (The song was one of my father's funniest and favorite concert pleasers.) The first verse, taken directly from the sign on a train goes: "Passengers will please refrain, from passing water, while the train is in the station, darling I love you." "If you need to pass some water, kindly call a Pullman porter, moonlight always makes me think of you....." Yes a Supreme Court Justice with a sense of humor!

So back in time we go, having gotten off track for a moment, I'm not sure if that's acceptable, but it's the way I think, so I figure as long as I keep you interested, it's OK.

My relationship with my father is still close to this day. I wouldn't be telling all these warm-hearted stories if it weren't. I'm not sure if this is just my nature to be extremely forgiving or if it's deserved. I have decided to err on the side of deserved, otherwise how could I possibly live with what was coming next?

Chapter Eleven

Looking back, it is hard to believe how many things were going on at once. I have recently been glued to YouTube watching my father's Canadian Show "Let's Sing Out," where so many important artists debuted. Many clips from that show have lately been used in documentaries about folk music: the earliest taped references available. Yes, we can read a book about these artists' debuts in the clubs in the Village. And there are some remarkable shots of famous people in photographs. But here on the black and white videos are the performers beginning their careers, and we can witness it so many years later.

I watched one recently with the Chapin Brothers, Dave Van Ronk, and Phil Ochs all on one stage. My favorite is always Joni Mitchell, probably because of all the ridiculous flirting going on. Much later, at the Mariposa Folk Festival in Toronto, I specifically remember a now well-known Joni after the show, backstage, flirting with Dad. As I approached them, I definitely remember getting the "stink-eye" from Ms. Mitchell, and my father asking me to take the boys back to the hotel. Doesn't take away one tiny little bit from her amazing talent and success. Just that I remember it like it was yesterday. About two years ago, I was sitting in a doctor's office and *People Magazine* had a screaming headline about the child Joni gave up for adoption at the beginning of her career. I tell you now, I grabbed that article and sighed relief when she spoke of her photographer husband and ill-timed pregnancy. I was glad she had a lovely reunion with her birth child, happy ending for everybody, including me.

Today these many documentaries and reminiscences flood the market because of the 50th anniversary of this or that famous moment; and echoes of my father ring throughout. For instance, today, September 20th, 2015, Judy Collins mentions Oscar Brand's radio show in a Facebook post, promoting her latest album. I look at all these footnotes with a nostalgic yet uneasy interest, because I remember the impact on my family, and wonder how things might have turned out if my father had been a better business man along with being a benevolent folksinger, willing to highlight and help everyone but himself. One thing I know for sure, he wouldn't mind at all. He would tell a great story and give himself a well-deserved pat on the back for helping a talented friend.

Oscar Brand and Joni Mitchell on "Let's Sing Out."
(Image courtesy Canadian Broadcasting Corporation.
Used by permission.)

The summers remained a great escape from the cramped apartment, and we travelled extensively in 1968 to every festival and even once again to Prince Edward Island. I confess that at the time I didn't think much about my friends who were stuck in the city. We never invited anyone on our trips. I may have had bragging rights at the time to exciting adventures, but I wasn't aware of it. So when school started again, so did the friendships and parties, just like before. We listened to music and I'm pretty sure that since my father never performed or even visited the school I attended, no one knew who he was.

It was about this time I decided I rather liked the fantasy of Judy Collins as a stepmother. I got this idea from how lovely she always looked, and of course how talented. But also because I saw such a nice affectionate rapport with my father. I'm sure they were just great friends, though I'll never know, because my fantasizing never equaled her remarkable journey. I was later surprised to read in her autobiography that she lost custody of her son because of a drinking problem. I guess you never know until you do.

Now I was in eighth grade. A teenager at last! Did this come with any special privileges? Well, since I already had a lot of freedom during the day, school seemed easy and my friendships were solid. I assumed this was going to be an exciting year.

My brothers had a few mandatory visits with my mother, which always left my brother Eric with a twitching eye, and I really don't remember how it affected my brother James. I wonder if he does. She by now had chosen to move to California with her ex-con. I suspect this was actually a dream come true for Dad, since he now only footed the bill and no longer had to deal with the trail of tears she left in her wake.

My apartment became a hangout for friends again. This was great because I wasn't walking home alone anymore. Too many challenging things had already happened. There were a lot of disturbing occurrences that left the girls pretty upset, like walking home from school one day when a man literally "flashed" my friend Dana and me. We were very upset. Question was what should I ask my father? Why did he do this? Again, being the wise man that he was, he put the blame on the man, of course, and told us he was a disturbed human being and this had nothing to do with us.

Why these odd things happened with Dana, I'm not sure. We stayed friends out of mutual need, but my friendship with Diana was actually closer. Diana was very, very pretty with long flowing brown hair and an exotic mixture of Hispanic and Irish good looks. Diana never went through the gawky teenager stage like I did, with my hair outrageously frizzed and a beanpole body. Diana was confident and smart. I liked being around her and her bohemian lifestyle.

Dana, on the other hand, was a blond bombshell, who resembled Cheryl Tiegs and blossomed very early. Dana and I were buddies. She always wanted a dad and that may have been the original reason for our closeness. Diana already had a father, but as previously mentioned, he rejected her and her attempts to be part of his new family.

So I had a popular friend and a best friend. That made up for a lot. The gang had a party every weekend, so it was still the pairing off of everyone for making out, and my boyfriend who put his arm around me once in a while, giving me his Bar Mitzvah bracelet to signify we were going steady, and staying nice and shy, which was for the best after all I had been through.

The breaking point for me came one day after a school field trip. I had borrowed my brother's ball for an end of the year picnic. Wherever they decided to take us needed a school bus, so off we went. It was later, after everyone had departed to go home, that I looked at Dana and remembered that I left the ball on the bus.

We walked back to school and I found some kids playing with the ball on the street. Please, please tell me why I didn't choose to walk away. All I could think about was that it was my brother's ball. I asked for it back nicely.

Imagine *West Side Story* here, only insert East Side Story. There wasn't a chance in hell we were getting the ball – and we were now being chased for sport with a baseball bat. We ran, trying car doors along the way, found an open one and jumped in the back seat. We put our hands over our heads out of instinct and WHAM! Glass flying everywhere. They had broken the window with the bat and ran off.

The police showed up moments later and took us to the station. They questioned us like we had done something wrong, but actually what had happened was we had stumbled on a gang that had been harassing kids and they needed names. Well, we recognized the kids from school, but we didn't name a single one and no one got into any trouble. There was an unspoken calm now at school. Word got out that we didn't snitch and we were left alone after that. Good deed or not, I cannot tell you, but I was my father's daughter in that moment, and no one was getting into trouble on my say so.

From those crazy days to the present, I have always made friends easily and kept them for life. Even when I became an adult, I retained my childhood friends, I think this is because I realize that everyone is insecure about something, and I always meet a new person with a compliment and a smile. This is a trait I inherited from my father, although as I look back at all the charming videos and clips, he is funny and witty, yet a bit of a wise guy. This is a trait I try not to emulate. Likeability is so important. I know my father was very well liked, but that may have had more to do with his power than his likable personality.

Most frustrating of all, for my family, even back in the days when I was unaware of how much Dad contributed to keeping the folk flame alive, was the lack of recognition he always struggled with. If you look on Wikipedia, his biography lists his awards: Emmy, Peabody, Curator of the Songwriter's Hall of Fame, television appearances, etc. But when I read biographies of the people he showcased on his programs or in concerts, they often neglect to mention him. Maybe it's a copyright thing, or maybe an oversight, who knows? But it is very upsetting

The lack of recognition has had financial implications. We were always chasing down people who used his work without paying for it. For instance, I watched a movie and the opening soundtrack was a song my father had written. Call a lawyer! *Oh, sorry! We thought that was an old American folk tune. Here's a check.* A cartoon comes on. Hey, wait a minute, they are using Dad's theme song from an old show. Call a lawyer! *Oops! Here's a check!* This happened so often that we assumed there must be many more times, but we just didn't know.

Arlo Guthrie tells a great story about his first day of kindergarten. He says everyone was singing "This Land is Your Land" and he was the only kid who didn't know the words! Big laugh, but copyright covered. When Arnold Schwartznegger walked into a class of school children in the movie "Kindergarten Cop" they were singing "When I First Came to This Land." My father wrote that song for his father as a tribute, although it is listed in many books as an old German folk tune. I assure you it is not. *Check please!*

There's another great, and completely true, story my father always likes to tell in concert. He begins by saying "This is my favorite song. The Smothers Brothers did a cover of it on their television show. It is called 'My Old Man's a Sailor.'"

The song, which my father wrote, is a children's song that gets more complex as it goes along, and the audience is supposed to keep singing along. It's very funny and keeps everyone laughing, including any back up musicians who find it impossible to keep up until the end, when everyone is hysterical. When the Smothers Brothers did it, they added a verse where Tommy Smothers says, "My old man's a Negro." The censors went wild. As usual, the always-daring Smothers Brothers had crossed a line. The Smothers Brothers show was so progressive for it's time that it was absolutely doomed to be cancelled. They later performed that same song on *The Tonight Show*. When a DVD was released after Johnny Carson's death, there were Tommy and Dick singing Dad's song. Dad got a whopping royalty, and has introduced it as his favorite song ever since.

I loved so many of the artists he showcased on his annual

Cooper Union Great Hall celebration. I remember people in the Green Room backstage, laughing and singing, very relaxed, making contacts, eating. In general, it didn't seem stressful or micro-managed the way things are today. I was just a little girl and no one stopped me from going back and forth, running errands, saying hi. Everyone just knew everyone else, although thinking back, there weren't other children backstage. Maybe Jean Ritchie's boys, but that's because they played alongside her, as is the family tradition.

One year, there were so many people that showed up, because the radio station gave away tickets for free and announced the date on Dad's show, that there was almost a riot outside. The show was showcasing extremely famous people all in one place, on one night, for free! My father told the police, who were beginning to gather to control the crowd, to let everyone in. Ticket or not, they could sit on the floor, as long as they didn't block the aisles or exits. This kind of informal solution could never happen today; and that's a shame.

I believe, if I'm truly honest, that might have been my favorite concert of all. I remember Pete Seeger warming up behind the curtain as Frank Warner and his sons finished their set. Everyone loved the comradery and no one fussed. It was hot and the air was thick, but the love was there. I adore my Rock just as much as anyone, but there is never a frenzy at a folk concert. No one ever pushes or shoves, they just sing along, and their voices blend in a lovely harmony. It's everything that is right with the world. *Kumbaya.*

Just this past month, Arlo Guthrie performed near my home town. We've recently reconnected on social media. Sometimes I might get a text, or I'll text him to give him a heads-up when and old interview with him is going to be re-aired on Dad's show. Very cordial and sweet man with so many children and grandchildren and still on the road. Now – as I write – he is doing the 50th Anniversary Tour for *Alice's Restaurant.*

I bought front row tickets to the show, and figured I'd text Arlo to let him know I was coming. Nothing pushy, just: *If you're up for it, I'd like to say hi.* I even extended an invitation to stay at my home, in case he wasn't into another night on a bus. Didn't hear back. Okay, that's fine; he's busy, tired, etcetera. Then the night of the show I get a text message on my phone. *Is tonight the night you're coming?* I said *yes* and he said: *OK, see you there.* I had no idea what that meant, and I was going with my husband and friends, so I just went.

Of course I enjoyed the show. His daughter Sarah Lee Guthrie was performing with him and sang a Phil Ochs song called "When I'm Gone" that could break your heart. Then she closed with an original song, written for her recently-deceased mother, and there wasn't a dry eye in the house, including mine. By the time Arlo came out to sing a shortened but funny "Alice" with a backdrop of the old movie behind him, the night had turned to magic.

Once the ovations had dissipated and everyone began to leave, I decided to check the security list and see if I was on it for a backstage hello. Guess what? I was the ONLY name on the list and he had been waiting for me on his bus. The other bus with his band had already left on its way to the next gig. It was a nice reunion, a big bear hug, but I could tell how tired he was, and I knew from years of experience to tell him how wonderful the show was and how much everyone enjoyed it.

I reminded him of a great photograph in which he figures that I have hanging over my desk called "Finale at Newport." This is from the very night he performed that famous song fifty years ago. It sparked an enormous reaction that I didn't expect. We really bonded over the fact that so much of our father's photos are owned by other people. I said I would try to get him a copy. I won't give up. A promise is a promise.

Later that night, I kept thinking even with all the money and fame, he still can't get or even collect a photo of such a pivotal moment in his life. I am deeply indebted to people like Frank Beacham and Chuck Morse of the World Folk Music Association, because they always allow me to use their photographs when promoting or texting about my father. That's the spirit that I was brought up to respect. People helping people, not for profit or personal gain, but because it is the right thing to do.

"Finale at Newport" in 1967. Arlo Guthrie near center with Oscar to Arlo's immediate left. (Photo by George Pickow.)

The rest of my conversation with Arlo will remain private. He is a spiritual guy, and that rubs off. I'm so glad we connected. Hugs all around before I stepped off the bus. The motor started. The bus headed on its way. And I walked off into a very foggy night alone, to my car, thinking about legacy.

I saw on Facebook a few weeks later a most perfect moment captured in a photograph by Arlo's daughter, Sarah Lee Guthrie. The tour had taken them to Tulsa, Oklahoma, and the Woody Guthrie Museum. The photo shows Arlo, grabbing a showcase of glass which contains his father's guitar. Arlo has his hands wrapped around the showcase as if to shake loose the past. Just touch it, feel it, play it again, but even he is not permitted. It's in a museum for posterity and he has the memories, just like I do. Still, it just doesn't seem right somehow. I shared the photo on my personal page. I believe I got the most "likes" of any post I have shared so far.

The other night I was listening to Dad's program which happened to be an archive show of the Weavers doing a tribute to immigration in the form of songs from other lands. Very relevant because of the Columbus Day holiday, and Dad, always in touch with what's happening in America, making his own statement by repeating this broadcast from 1955. Just proving that change is what America was built on, and the songs and people, except of course the indigenous people, all came from somewhere else. Including of course, my Dad, which is why this is such an important issue to him.

Somewhere, buried in all the banter, was a little throwaway sentence about how Lee Hays had approached my father with the idea of forming the group which became The Weavers. Lee explained to Dad that this would be a tightly disciplined, well-rehearsed endeavor. When my father heard the word "disciplined," he promptly refused to join and suggested Pete Seeger. The rest is history, and another opportunity missed. Again, I'm sure this was never a problem for my father. He couldn't have been happier for their success, and interviewed them many times, promoting them on his show constantly. On their very first appearance, they asked listeners to call in to WNYC with suggested names for their new quartet. The Weavers became *The Weavers*, right on Dad's program. (Many years later, at the ceremony where Dad received his Peabody Award for Individual Broadcasting, they played the tape of that show, along with Bob Dylan's first radio interview.)

To end this chapter, and going back to the theme of immigration, here's a favorite – and somewhat fantastic – story about coming to America that my father likes to refer to as "the tale of my father's first job." In Canada, my grandfather worked for a time as an interpreter to the Hudson's Bay Trading Company. The joke of course, as my father tells it, is that my grandfather couldn't speak the native-American's lanaguage, but the latter couldn't tell that to the Hudson's Bay Company except through my grandfather! Of course, this is a silly exaggeration, but it gets a laugh every time. I think back to little nuanced experiences with my father, say at a restaurant, when he would try to guess and pinpoint where a waiter might be from just by his or her dialect, and then of course sing a little song for them from their native land. Always a people pleaser, and a charmer; we learned well at his knee.

On the occasion of Folksong Festival's 50ᵗʰ Anniversay broadcast, 1995.
Left to right: Pete Seeger, Oscar Brand, Josh White Jr., and Odetta.
(Brand Family Collection.)

Chapter Twelve

Now, as they used to say on the old T.V. shows, back to our story. Routine became the saving grace, since – for obvious reasons – there were no more trips to mothers for anyone.

We all settled in, Dana's cat had kittens, we sneaked them into the apartment from time to time. Of course I fell in love with one and begged for it. My father relented with a note that said, "Keep it, Daddy," which I still have in the little box of memories that actually survived. Kitty litter in the kitchen, but purring on the bed. I developed a lifelong habit of rescuing and loving animals: the little mother in me. Unfortunately, this particular cat had a habit of going out the fire escape by the kitchen window, so eventually we lost him to "Tom Catting," which is why all my cats for the next 50 years were female, including the one by my side right now, Pandora. Aptly named, because I adopted her, along with the idea of writing this book, not knowing what I was going to release to the world. We decided the truth was way better than anything in my imagination.

Okay, yes, I'm stalling. I have to organize into a viable page how the next chapter will come about, and it's daunting. So take a deep breath, tell the truth, and "away we go!" (Quoting Jackie Gleason here.)

The reason for the trepidation I believe, is that 1969 may have been the catalyst to so many changes. First let's start with an amazing experience at the end of the previous summer. PBS had a special series where Dad would travel to historic sites of the past and sing the songs of the people who built America. I remember Williamsburg of course, and the usual historical sites like Gettysburg, but the one that stands out as my favorite memory was Hershey, PA. Of course you think any child would love Chocolate town, U.S.A. But although we visited the attractions and the factory for fun, the reason for this episode was a lot darker than the chocolate. It was an episode about coal mining. Just a short distance away from all the fun and glamour, was a tiny abandoned mining town, exactly like your imagination would think. Grey and dusty and deserted, completely derelict and not a sole survivor. Reminds me of all the songs Merle Travis would sing about the mines such as "Dark as a Dungeon," with its haunting lyrics … or Jean Ritchie's "The L&M Don't Stop Here Anymore."

The story was set in one of the real houses and for fun I was dressed as a coal miner's daughter, seriously, to pretend to serve beans and coffee to the miners before they headed out, as my father sang the songs. It wasn't my acting debut, but pretty close. I don't count the other little girl extra parts, that I basically can't remember.

What made this so memorable was that the lights for the inside of the cold, dark cabin had to be extra bright for the cameras. As we went into *take three*, I could see that the back of one of the doors was bubbling, but I wasn't allowed to speak during a take. Well, it happened. The door caught fire! It was very exciting and the last time I held my tongue when I noticed something amiss. Good life lesson.

Autumn 1968. All too soon it was back to school: Grade Seven. Next year it would be time for to start applying to High Schools. You see, in New York City the public High Schools – except for very few – were abysmal. So the competition for private High Schools, or for the better public High Schools, was as tough as college. I wasn't really thinking much about that in the fall of 1968. I was just studying hard and doing my best. Eventually my boyfriend would be accepted to Stuyvesant High, one of the best public schools in the city and the toughest academically. But the biggest surprise was that my friend Diana also was accepted. She'd be was one of the first trailblazing girls to enter this formerly all boys' high school. The doors and opportunities were opening up for women. She was so smart, and beautiful, what a terrible waste. We never knew her demons would overtake her, and by the time I got that last call, it was too late. I could not imagine a future in which she would fall in love with an older man, then lose him and sink into a profound depression. I wasn't immedaiately available in person, and she didn't call. Either way, she succeeded in ending her life. But this was still yet to come.

You might wonder why I wasn't available for my best friend. Truth be told, it was because I had once again been lifted out of my life physically and geographically. And now that story unfolds, with an end in sight to all the drama, or so I thought.

The spring of 1969 was such an exciting time for my father. The newly formed Songwriter's Hall of Fame was housed at One Times Square. (It's the building where the ball drops every year on New Year's Eve). On the original board of directors were my Dad and also his good friends Johnny Mercer and Howie Richmond of The Richmond Organization (TRO) music publishing house. This was one of the most amazing places to visit. Besides hosting tributes and induction ceremonies every year, there were also plenty of parties and a place to exhibit rare items related to great songwriters of the past. (Even Judy Garland's ruby slippers had a place in a display, because after all *The Wizard of Oz* was a musical!)

No steadfast rules. Just a neat place to explore; and my father had an office and a secretary like a regular job. Of course, a non-paying one, but I think that probably goes without saying by now.

I continued my babysitting duties and branched out to actually making a few dollars babysitting for real for some neighbors. So I had a little pocket money. This was strange and wonderful. A teenage girl with some pocket change, no role model to show me what I needed or what to buy, for fashion accessories, but I did get my friend Dana to iron my crazy curly hair, so I looked a lot better.

Come the summer, we once more headed off to our round of festivals. There was a big shift in the festivals that year and even I could tell that folk/rock was becoming the norm. Most of the people performing had records out and the crowd was definitely younger, and the music louder and less traditional than what I had grown up with.

Of course, the most memorable night of that summer was when Neil Armstrong and Buzz Aldrin landed on the moon. I was backstage at the Newport Folk Festival, along with so many other people, crowded around a small black and white television, while onstage James Taylor tried to finish his set.

When the landing was announced, the crowd roared and applauded wildly. I will never forget the excitement. One of only two times I saw my father cry with joy. The other was when they elected President Obama, something he thought he would never live to see. Many years after the moon landing, James Taylor appeared at the newly restored Newport Folk Festival to – as he put it – "finish his set."

We also went to the wonderful Mariposa Festival in Ontario, Canada.

Yes, we drove, singing all the way. I liked this festival because the actual stage was set on an island in an amusement park. You had to take a little ferry back and forth to the mainland and the hotel. Quite an adventure and loads of fun because for the first time I was liberated from taking care of my brothers. I can't remember why, but I was assigned to help a pregnant Joan Baez get around the festival. The little ferry boat was a bit of a challenge, but I remember that she was so sweet to me, especially knowing now that her husband was in jail, for refusing to be drafted as a protest against the Vietnam War. I spent the next few days helping her get food, walking with her everywhere. And the boat! I'll never forget that little boat. It seemed to tip when we got in! I still think that it was so gracious of her to keep her promise to perform, even though she could have easily backed out. And because she was so famous by that time, it helped to make the Festival a success, which was good for the local performers.

After Mariposa, we had one more stop on the Festival round, and that was Philadelphia. I fell for Dave Van Ronk at that one. Not in a teenage crush way, but musically. This man was such a paradox. He was, to me, big and burly and rough. But when he sang a song called "Thyme (It is a Precious Thing)," the roughness melted away and transformed him in a way that touched my soul. I adore so many songs and have heard so many performances in my life, but I will never forget that particular night or that song. It truly stands alone as my musical awakening. I understood why people travelled great distances for one artist. It's a mystical craving we all have inside, but although we all have partially fulfilled it on occasion, rarely is it completely satisfied.

So now, back in the Village apartment, the last year of Junior High: Eighth Grade. Music became our focus. Like most teenagers, the Beatles consumed us still, and we listened and danced in the dark at parties. I wish I could tell you I noticed something going on with my father, but I didn't. Was he whistling more, was he happier? Can't say. All I know is that one Sunday evening we were headed to WNYC for his weekly broadcast, expecting to see GG, right after, for dinner.

We found a young woman – introduced as *Karen* – sitting up front in the car waiting for us. I was in the backseat, and for the 15 minutes it took to drive downtown, I started to notice things. Her hair was a dark brown, stylish flip, sprayed into submission. She seemed to be about 35 to me, because of her sophisticated clothes and gold jewelry. Really put together. Except for a habit of twirling a lock of hair, she seemed very calm. When we pulled into the municipal parking lot, Dad instructed us to stay in the car while he did his broadcast.

OK. So I guess we'll talk to the mystery woman. She had toys and puzzles for my brothers, and that was nice. I admired her turtleneck sweater, and she immediately said she'd take me shopping. This sounded promising. More than a little exciting too. Then she came with us for dinner with Grandma, and I got it. This was serious. The reason dad was never home on weekends. The reason he was happy again. He was having a love affair. I was trying to fill in the blanks, but I had no idea how far it would go.

His career was stalled as far as performing – a fact which made being admired by a young woman all the more enticing. Little did I know that this was the woman who had fallen for him at Grossingers, when she was fourteen. By the time we met, she was actually 24 years old. She'd been married and divorced, and she was my father's biggest fan.

True to her word, the next time we met she took me shopping on Fifth Avenue. We went to the Godiva Chocolate Shop, the only one that existed at the time. It was like a jewelry store for chocolate, and beautiful. Next stop, Bergdorf Goodman where we bought a turtleneck exactly like the one I'd admired. This was good, I liked this gal a lot. I learned that she had gone to the University of Pennsylvania, and that she was currently attending law school at Villanova. So being a smart girl, I put the pieces together and guessed that she came from money and that she took the train on weekends to N.Y. to meet my Dad at a fancy hotel. On her dime, and probably a nice change for Dad.

I will never forget Thanksgiving at her family's fine home in Philadelphia. I can't imagine what her mother and father were thinking. I know they were gracious and lovely and accepting on the surface. But I felt an undercurrent of Charles Dickens even at that first meeting.

Consider the man at your beautiful home, introducing his basically three orphaned children: a man twice your daughter's age, a man twice divorced, and a folksinger. Probably not what they had in mind for their only daughter. We ate dinner and I specifically remember going upstairs to use the bathroom, which was bigger than my bedroom, and secretly hoping this would work out. Anything was better than how we lived, and there was no way that this pretty young girl, who dressed so stylishly, showing a little more cleavage than necessary, but still elegant, was going to live in a dive on Perry Street.

Right on Jeannie, but not entirely the way you planned it.

I swear the next part is true. I had long hair, for which my soon to be stepmother bought an elegant hair ornament. I cut off all my hair, into a short bob. Why? I don't know. An act of rebellion, probably. Things were moving way too fast. On one hand, she being Dad's biggest fan seemed nice for him, and the idea of being a normal teenager without the responsibilities of the boys – wow. What could be better than that? I just thought we would have more time.

We were scheduled to go to Canada again. Apparently, I found out later, the lovers couldn't stand the thought of being separated; so they set a wedding date before the trip - with a promise to her father that she would finish law school after they were married. Wise man, her father.

So the next time I saw her was at her parents' country club for our wedding. I call it *our* wedding, because we all stood up on the podium together. I remember my brother James at five, just a cutie pie and clueless. Eric had a bad toothache and never smiled. And I looked all arms and legs, with my short curly hair with a giant bow. Karen, of course, looked spectacular in a green Lavin dress with a bow in back and the helmet of hair that never moved. We took a family wedding photo. My father was the only one really smiling. Karen was as regal as a queen who had married her prince, but actually considering the age difference (she had just turned 25 and Dad was 50) more like marrying the king. A scandal indeed, but not uncommon in the entertainment business. We all had high hopes. And we all headed north to Canada, on my father's honeymoon.

Life was moving fast. Too fast. And many of us were growing up too fast. My friend Dana – who helped us pack the car for Canada – had just moved in with her 15-year-old boyfriend in his bedroom at his parents' house. Change was the only constant. And little did I know my brothers and I were about to be upheaved one more time.

Chapter Thirteen

Happily ever after is the way to end fairy tales. I could put any kind of spin on the next few years that I wish. So far it's been the truth, and I think I will just go with that.

Upon our arrival at Prince Edward Island, we found ourselves in the same house as the last three years. Same gig. And with his new bride by his side, every night that Dad performed I was left behind to babysit the boys. This was new. At least before there had been music and people as we wandered backstage. Now I was alone in a dark, lonely house by the sea, with monsters inside to care for and outside to be afraid of. Can't imagine it was pleasant for the young Mrs. Brand either: three kids on your honeymoon, one old enough to know what was going on behind closed doors. (Frankly, there were no ceilings on the rooms, so peering over the top of a wall was fun for my brothers. Maximum *icky* factor.)

Here's what I didn't know at the time. A deal had been made between my father and new stepmother. He would keep his money, children, and past separate; she would do the same. An impossible task, even with the best intentions, but they decided this was a good idea.

Upon our return from Canada we went not to Perry Street, but rather to a "good school district" in the town of Great Neck, Long Island. A traveling professor and his family had left their furnished house for one year, and this was a perfect place for us to rent while while Dad and Karen shopped for a permanent home. Of course, a gawky teenager thrust into 9th grade with a bunch of strangers in a village called *Lake Success* was not going to fair well. In fact, it was almost culture shock.

From the Greenwich Village of the 60's to the "Hollywood East" of New York's "Gold Coast." The only redeeming factor was the close proximity to my godmother Jean, who still lived in the very "low key" and nearby Port Washington, where we visited often and felt more connected to our past.

There was a strange German housekeeper who came with our house. She lived in the attic, was straight out of a *B* horror movie. Everything was the Master's decision. When she cleaned the floors, we couldn't walk on them until my father got home to inspect them. She scared the crap out of me and my brothers. (As it turns out, I later learned she liked and was much happier with us than with the professorial family. So she decided to come along with us a year later when we moved to the brand-new Brand house. But all I knew for sure was that she terrified me, and I did all I could to stay clear of her wrath.

Try to imagine a house that is filled with someone else's furniture. The closets too. No room for your stuff – even though since we didn't have much, it wasn't really an issue. Just weird. Like being on a movie set, but you lived there. After one week, I was asked to exchange rooms with my brother because I was too close to the folks, and might hear something.

After a few months of babysitting, being bullied at school by mean girls who didn't GET my Bohemian clothing, and never attending even one of the music events that I used to cherish, I had had enough. This wasn't the dream come true I was expecting. So I did a very foolish thing. I took off in search of *you-know-who*, and no one tried to stop me.

I took a plane to California, Marina del Ray in fact. It was gorgeous and appealing. I spent just one night in my mother's apartment before all hell broke loose again. She was stunningly drunk and abusive, accusations flying in the middle of the night, and again, I was tossed out. But this time, I was alone, way across the country, with only $40.00 and a ticket to New York, booked for a flight a week away. No walking home in the middle of the night in familiar territory. This was serious. No cellphones or computers or a credit card. Only my wits and a need to get in touch with Dad, because he'd know what to do, I hoped.

I remember a cab ride to a hotel in downtown Los Angeles. I

actually told the cab driver my predicament; so he took me as close to the airport as possible and refused fare. Good man. Could have turned out to be a terrible choice, so far, so good.

There was a big hotel and I asked the desk clerk if it was possible to call my father long distance, so I could stay over. I didn't look like a hooker, although that's what I had been accused of only hours before by my own mother. I just looked like a frightened teenage girl in a red tube top, jeans and sandals

It was pretty much early morning by the time they reached Dad on the East Coast. Hearing my total panic, he came up with an idea. *Have a vacation Jeannie!* Turn this around and make it a good thing. Go to Disneyland! He'd work on changing my ticket and pay the hotel by VISA. This was a great relief. god bless them, they took the card over the phone. So then I caught the bus to Disneyland, with $40 still in my purse and a great adventure ahead of me.

Boy, do I want to tell you that this turned out well. Really I do. But at 15, alone, I was prey. I'd been lucky so far, but now I became all too trusting. Never made it to Disneyland. A "nice" young boy sat next to me on the bus. He said he was a runaway. What did I know? He suggested we get off the bus before Disneyland, and visit Knott's Berry Farm. And so we did, and went on a few rides together. I was such an easy mark. I thought he was my age. He reminds me in my memory of Brad Pitt in the movie "Thelma and Louise," taking advantage of my naivety.

He actually wore a cowboy hat. I trusted that. Dad wore them too. After a day of fun, I tried to shake him and I couldn't. I decided to head back to the hotel, certainly they would help me out there.

I had a room, a key, and luggage. He was glued to me like a puppy. I guess I felt sorry for the sob story or something, I knew I was going home to a family and he had nowhere to sleep, so I said *OK, sleep on my floor.* Reading this, you are saying to yourself: I know what's going to happen next. You're right, so I won't write it. It was awful and embarrassing, and fortunately he left for whatever reason, and I locked the door. When he returned later, banging on the door for me to let him in, I called security. After that, I don't know what happened to him.

I left for New York the next day, making sure to buy a souvenir for my little brother, promising myself I'd remember that no matter how bad things might get at home, it was better than the alternative. It's been 45 years since that trip. I've never seen my mother again. Many years later I heard that she suffered from Agoraphobia, the fear of leaving one's home. If I had known that I might have felt safer; instead I was always waiting for some call or emergency that never came.

I recently had the opportunity to ask my stepmother what she thought about those early days. She answered that she thought my only concern was whether I could keep my cat, otherwise I was OK with the whole deal.

She was pretty young and so I can see where she might only be concerned with her new role as Mrs. Oscar Brand and making a perfect home for my father. I get that. Probably, a built in babysitter worked just fine for her. I don't think she was aware at all how much of a culture shock my siblings and I were going through. I didn't blame her at all, yet.

By the end of the school year, the folks – that's how I refer to them to this day – found a house on a hill on the other side of town. This was and is, a great house. The first of its kind in the "Old Money" part of town. It is a Spanish Stucco, flat roof, six bedroom, five bathroom display of architectural wonder built in the 1930's to resemble the great houses of Hollywood. The basement had a projection room, really cool. There were also three fireplaces, maid quarters with a separate entrance, and a room we just called "The Blue Room" because of all the fresco artwork.

Best of all, there were beautiful stained glass windows and Italian mosaic artwork in each bathroom. The people who sold it to my father were divorcing, so he bought it under market and move-in ready.

As previously mentioned, the housekeeper came along too,

although she refused to live in the servant's quarters, which I thought odd. So she took over the blue room. The first of many household guests that came for a few days and stayed for months. Dad's influence to be sure. I ended up in the servant's quarters – but I'm sure you could have guessed that by now.

The house boasted a classic 1970's color scheme. Every room was painted in brilliant colors: lime green, orange, yellow, etc. Also a red living room and dining room with the heavy red and black drapes. Over the years the house has become blonde. All color stripped as each of us moved on or out. The only remains of this movie set of a house is "The Blue Room" still and to this day.

About now you are starting to wonder why bother to go on? Sounds like everything turned out great. And I thought so too. I had a new school to go to, old money, kids comfortable with it, no shaming. I had seemed to blossom overnight (probably due to a prescription for endometriosis, which included birth control pills), grown my hair long, wore tight jeans or hot pants.

First day of school, someone mistook me for a very popular girl. Her name was Maddie. As soon as I was introduced, I was immediately accepted into her clique of friends. I went into the city as often as I could to meet my boyfriend, who says he was around for a sweet sixteen party at the house that I can't remember. But I certainly was popular at school. Didn't hurt that Dad performed there and I became a pseudo-celebrity. (After that people were always asking if I knew Bob Dylan or Pete Seeger to the point where it was irritating, because there were so many other talented people I knew well; but of course, to teenagers in the '70s those were the names.)

My stepmother transferred to Hofstra Law School to complete her graduate degree. I was oblivious to how hard she was working, and of course a little jealous again of all the cool concerts and benefits she attended with Dad. But one night my father came to me for a discussion. An important one that I will never forget. This was absolutely the pivotal point in his marriage, and its success was my responsibility.

With tears in his eyes (he was genuinely worried) he said, "Jeannie, if you don't keep those boys away from Karen, I will be divorced again, and we will end up back in the city and poor."

Ahh yes - *the pact*. It wasn't only about money; it was about the separation of family. I agreed to do my best, and I did. The trajectory had changed again. Panic had set in; and it was all up to me to make things better. Not fair. A giant burden I should never have been asked to carry. On the other hand, I had finally found some sense of belonging, I liked the house, the school, the social life. I wasn't giving that up without a fight.

Early Seventies.

Chapter Fourteen

By now, the boys were in school. Because of our age difference we never were in the same school at the same time. I left a pretty good reputation behind me in High School: teachers liked me, I did well and participated in theater groups. My brother Eric, who later followed me, was an out-standing personality so he didn't experience any trouble either. My brother James, well, I will get to that later.

We celebrated every occasion with the Pickows. Now both Thanksgiving and Christmas were at Jean's house. The Seder's were at ours. Jean's sons were by now singing with her; they became an integral part of the folk scene at a young age, on hand for many performances. Meanwhile, Oscar's children stayed home – although every once in a while I was able to tag along.

In 1972, Mayor John V. Lindsay of New York, decided he would run for President and had a campaign fund raiser. He asked Dad to come and perform. and I went too, being sixteen and suddenly very politically conscious. (OK. Lindsay was handsome and charismatic, and I really wanted to go. Fine.) When we arrived at the party it was already late and noisy. I really hate noise. Love music, can't take noise, so I stood in a corner and a young man came up to me with the saddest face I'd seen in a long time. Wounded in a way. He was very tall and had to slump over to talk to me. (I'm 5'6" … so you see he was *really* tall!) We tried to talk. I'm a sucker for people in trouble, and I think I can fix everything with a kind word, but I couldn't really hear him, so he invited me for a cup of coffee around the corner. I think it was the famous Carnegie Deli. Anyway, we sat in a booth while he poured his broken heart out to me over his breakup with his longtime girlfriend. I listened. He was a struggling actor, of course, and really heartbroken. The next time I saw him was years later on the big screen playing *Superman*. It was Christopher Reeve.

I've had a few brushes with the famous, even without being the daughter of a famous father, we all have, especially if you live in New York or Los Angeles. But my favorite story happened about two years later when I was walking down Fifth Ave. In the 1970's, if you were a dark haired girl, you tanned. It's just what we did. We didn't know how bad it was for us. I tanned dark and wore the filmy fun blouses that got attention at concerts. On this day, I decided to throw a few flowers into the mix and scattered them through my long black hair.

I think I was going to a movie with the boyfriend of the moment. A parade of people were coming straight towards us marching down Fifth Avenue; they weren't chanting anything, and it was really quiet. No one was afraid. Lots of protest of the war in Vietnam were under my belt by now, and they could turn very violent and scary, or be peaceful on moratorium days, it depended on the sponsors. But this was different. The crowd seemed to get bigger as it got closer and I could see it was made up entirely of people of color. Right smack in the middle of the first line of people was a giant of a man. He walked right towards me, and held out his hand and touched the flowers, saying, "You have beautiful hair." I recognized him immediately. It was Mohammed Ali, and he was going to the premiere of his movie "The Greatest" – the large crowd of admirers tagging behind. After that, I was a fan too. All the fuss of changing his name, and religion, refusing to serve, being perhaps the greatest boxer in history. In my mind, he liked me, so I liked him. Simple as that.

Now life is sounding pretty good right? High school was fun. We had a stable, functioning home. Well, that depends on what you call stable and functioning. Dad still had the habit of collecting and helping people who were down on their luck, and this time it was the Reverend Bill Glenesk. Does that name sound familiar? He was the man who had married Tiny Tim and Miss Vicki live on the Tonight Show with Johnny Carson. He also worked with my father on a limited edition album called "Celebrate." When the good Reverend lost his congregation in the Village, Dad gave him a temporary place to stay, and he stayed temporarily for 9 months on our couch. Actually, this wasn't very disruptive, at least not for us. There were always so many people coming and going, sometimes a spillover from Jean's and George's, or sometimes just a stop in the states for travelling musicians. This part of my father's life was not negotiable. My stepmother had to say *yes*, and she did. Later some of her family joined us and also stayed.

Big house, lots of room, just the kids feeling the squeeze. But I had lots of friends, and because as the boys grew a bit older I didn't need to be a constant presence at home, I got an afterschool job at the local jewelry store. The goal was to buy my own car. Independence, thy name is *car*.

I approached the task of getting employment very pragmatically. Great Neck is really a small town. I got all dressed up. Started at one end of town, and walked into every shop until I found an old jewelry store, run by a man who was second generation, and willing, if I got working papers, to hire me from 3-6pm every weekday and Saturdays. Perfect. With papers in order, and an actual mentor in an older girl who worked there full time, let's call her *Randy*, I was ready for my new career. Of course this meant dressing up a little extra special at school, so it was noticed. No one else had an afterschool job, but it added to the mystery of the folksinger's daughter and actually made me more popular.

There are all sorts of benefits to having a famous father, but sometimes sneaky life situations make that distinction a distraction. One year we went to a political fundraiser on Long Island where Dad was advertised in the local paper as the entertainment. How convenient for the thieves who knew we wouldn't be home all afternoon and ransacked the house. Not finding anything but MY small stash of jewelry, they sprayed the house with graffiti. Not long after we got an alarm system. I hated it. Still do. It's an awful way to live. I suppose the crooks were disappointed. Maybe from the outside the house looked grand, but it was mostly filled with instruments and paintings that are easily identified and hard to fence.

Anyway, so now I was a working girl – accidently stepping into what would become my career. I liked the job. No one ever comes into a jewelry store in a bad mood. (I made that line up; and have worked in the field ever since, always using that phrase.) I like people and already knew many of the people who walked through the door; so I was pretty successful at sales right away.

There was only one problem. The owner of the store was a real letch. The counter was tightly fit to the wall and this man would rub up against me as he passed from counter to counter. I felt him; it was disgusting. So I asked my mentor Randy about it. Her reply: "Yeah, he does that, but it's harmless." Today it would be sexual harassment. Back then it was just part of the job.

Wish I could write that this was the only problem, but there was also a watchmaker, no surprise here. I thought he would be sympathetic, but instead he would tell me his dream from the night before which always included some warped fantasy about me. I really can't fathom how I stayed. I just think that with everything I had already been through, this was pretty small on the scale of what to put up with on a daily basis. I didn't know that it wouldn't happen everywhere, so I stayed three years.

My first purchase was a little black and white T.V. set. Wow total independence to have your own set, but the next one was the big one. At sixteen, rich kids got a car for their birthdays. I didn't expect that, but I also wanted my own car. Dad taught me to drive on a gigantic Chrysler New Yorker. The car that went to Canada and back three times. It was like driving a boat. Easy, but one wrong move and it could destroy anything in its path. I was allowed to borrow it if I waited on the gas lines in the early mornings before school. Not everyone remembers those times, but there was an oil embargo, the rules were that you could fill your tank if you were more than half empty and only on odd or even days, depending on your license plate. Our family had two cars, with NBC 53 and NBC 54 plates. Lucky for us, and convenient to parking at 30 Rockefeller center. Even though Dad no longer had a show, the license plates were cool.

When I finally got my own car, it was a disaster, albeit a hilarious disaster. A little old lady, who I worked with at the store, and who lived two blocks away, had a car that she never drove, ever. Laughing yet? I bought her car for $400 and proceeded to put every dime I earned into that car. The car hadn't been driven in so long that every hose broke, and always on a highway or inconvenient spot. I eventually came to hate that car.

Actually, it was a love/hate relationship, because it was a 1964 Dodge Polara, with a push button transmission, which seemed to excite the guys. I didn't care, just wanted it to take me where I wanted to go, without having to beg permission from the folks for a loaner. And I didn't think, initially, that it would cost too much to fix up the Polara.

In those days, Earl Scheib in Long Island was like the Maaco of today. The company would advertise a ridiculously low price to have your car painted, and of course the add-ons were extra. Well, on my day off, determined to be driving at least an acceptable piece of hardware, I drove to get my $29.95 paint job. I was promptly informed that the rust on the doors and hood was so bad that it would probably run an additional $300 or more to remove. What did I do, besides burst into tears? I decided to go to the hardware store, buy some fine sandpaper and prep it myself.

And that's exactly what I did. Except I didn't go home. I drove right back to the paint shop and started sanding in the parking lot in full view of the workers. By the time a half an hour had gone by, I had no nails left, my fingers were bleeding, and the guys couldn't take it anymore. Or maybe it just looked bad for business. Anyway, they sanded my car by machine in about ten minutes and painted it, for free, with the admonishment never to tell anybody. Except of course I told everyone, because I only saw the generosity of what they had done for me.

Many years later, I sold that car to Jon Pickow for one dollar, on the condition that I would never hear of it or see it again. No such luck. This is the absolute truth. Jon ended up selling it to my brother Eric, who took it away to college with him, and drove it without oil one day or it would possibly still be on the road.

In 1974, with my graduation and the prospect of college looming on the horizon, I was pretty much on my own when it came to planning the next great adventure of my life.

By this time, Mr. and Mrs. Brand were completely wrapped up in their lives. The step-kids had a nice home, but we were basically boarders. This sounds mean and ungrateful, but it isn't meant to, just an explanation of how even with the great change in living arrangements, not much had changed. Dinner on the table every night. Sure. I remember lively discussions and lots of PDA, which wasn't appropriate and kind of an appetite killer; but Karen was a good cook, and there was always plenty of food. But I'm sure at every other kid's house there was a discussion about college. My New York boyfriend was heading to Harvard, a couple of nice guys I dated on and off, Yale, a few more Ivy Leaguers, and the rest to state schools. Everyone had somewhere to go. I didn't know about applications and interviews. Eventually I applied late to ten schools, all of them state schools – and took the interview trips myself.

Jean Ritchie's son was at Purchase. So I thought, *good, at least I'll know someone.* His cousin was at Stonybrook, so I applied there too. But the one I really wanted was New Paltz. It had a great art program and I loved art and literature, plus they were offering a partial scholarship.

Well I got into every school I applied to. Congratulations to me. Then I had the TALK with my father. He was actually upset with me for expecting that he would pay for my college education. I will never, ever, forget this conversation, because later in life he told me it was the biggest and only regret he had. At that time, his answer to me was that he had no money and refused to co-sign a loan. He never asked his wife for money, that was their deal; she could have offered, but didn't; and I could have asked, but didn't. So his advice was to do what he did: work my way through Brooklyn College, his alma mater, which he assured me he could get me into.

I took this information to my guidance counselor, but by then it was too late. The only option remaining was Kingsborough Community College, in the bowels of Brooklyn. I was completely devastated. Out of over 450 students who graduated that June, only two weren't going to college, and I was one of them. So much for fame and fortune.

I visited the campus once, and never got out of the parking lot. Since I would be working during the day and going to school at night, I recognized the signs of a dangerous situation. I made up my mind to take a year off, save my money, and go to Stonybrook on my own dime. I really wanted the experience, plus it was close enough to come home on weekends to work. I had another reason, and it involved my first serious relationship and that seemed like a good basis for my decision.

During my high school years, Carole King's *Tapestry* was the big hit album we played at parties – the parties where you broke up with the guy of the week and found someone else's heartbreak guy, who'd be yours until the following weekend. Simon and Garfunkel were who you sulked over your breakups with, and Loggins & Messina were the hot, concert, date night ticket.

Because Dad had helped out the producer of all those Madison Square Garden concerts, a guy named Ron Delsner, I believe, all he had to do was make a phone call and I had press box seats, or at least excellent ones. So I was good date material and saw all the big names of the '70s. The point is that I got to ask the guys I liked to go. It made me feel empowered and special not to have to wait to be asked, or miss a great time waiting to be invited. All that ended with everyone scattering for college.

But there was one last party, not my prom (which I attended with a college guy on my arm), but a little costume party. This party was given by the only couple I knew who dated and married right out of high school.

I dressed up as a pussycat. As soon as I arrived, I noticed that this wasn't the usual crowd. My friend from school had invited some "outsiders," guys from Brooklyn College. So, new people, and very exciting, especially since one of them – dressed as a train engineer, buff and without a shirt under the overalls – seemed to take an interest in me. A beautiful guy, great sense of humor, same taste in music, and available. He was smitten, and so was I. But honestly, the fact that he was commutable didn't hurt either.

We dated for a little over a year. I taught him to drive in my Polara. He was absolutely the funniest person I had ever met. And to this day, he is one of my brother's best friends, which should tell you how good I am at breakups.

It was with him that I saw an "emerging" talent at the Bottom Line. It was Billy Joel, before the release of the *Stranger* album. The club is a small intimate place; we sat at a table in the front row, and he knocked us out with his power and energy.

I have been to so many concerts, both intimate and huge. I sometimes feel so out of place buying an expensive ticket to sit in nosebleed seats, when I grew up in the green room, backstage. After a while, unless it was truly something special, I stopped going. It just felt too weird. I used to say, *If Dad's not on the bill, what's the point?*

This is not snobbery in any sense of the definition, it's just the way I grew up. I'm never intimidated to go backstage after a performance, no matter if I know the performer or not. I think that everybody in the audience is, in a way, their employer. If we didn't buy a ticket, they wouldn't have a gig. I saw Alan Arkin in a play off-Broadway and congratulated him on his performance. My date was stunned at the ease of my conversation, but of course I had met him in Croton as one of the "Shanty Boys", so to me he was approachable.

I remember one occasion when going backstage didn't work out so well. This was about thirty years ago. At a Kennedy Center concert, Gordon Lightfoot was visibly drunk on stage. My Dad had been the first to bring Gordon down from Canada, and played a big part in getting him started in his career. When I saw him backstage, I introduced myself as Oscar's daughter. Then he answered – and I'll never forget this - "Is that old man still alive?" Lovely. Good music, Gordon. Not a big fan.

Judy Collins, Oscar Brand, and Gordon Lightfoot on Oscar's Canadian television program. (Image Courtesy Canadian Broadcasting Corporation. Used by permission.)

It seems as if all the important transitions in my life are tied to having a celebrity father. Even the most difficult facts of life that everyone must face, like the death of a loved one.

This is the reason that the," train engineer" boyfriend will hold a place in my heart forever. He was working as a page for NBC when a new show called "Saturday Night Live' premiered. My grandmother, my father's mother had been suffering from dementia for a while, and the night she passed away, Rob, my boyfriend, had arranged for me to be in the audience for the taping of the show. I think that Dyan Cannon was hosting and Paul Simon and Art Garfunkel were the guests. It was terribly exciting. After it was over, we met my father outside in his station wagon with the entire family sitting inside.

My father broke the news to me that his mother had passed away and the funeral was the next day. I don't know how he could have been so strong, but he knew the news would be devastating and didn't want to spoil this one last happy night for me.

Except for Jean Ritchie, my grandma Bea was the closest to a mother figure I had. It was a rare and special gift from them both. I will never forget that kindness.

The irony here is that my stepmother believed in pedigree; when asked for advice, a rarity, she advised against the actor boyfriend in favor of the Ivy Leaguers. I'm thinking her heart was in the right place, but when acting didn't work out, he became a Madison Avenue dentist. And therein lies the irony.

Maybe it was youth, or searching for something more stable as well, but I took her advice and tagged along on a few, "opportunities" to meet the right type of man. Of course still a little strange coming from a person married to a folksinger with three children, but I was still young enough not to recognize that paradox. I wasn't thinking about a good match; at that age, you think about an exciting adventure!

One evening we had an invitation to another star-studded dinner; I doubt it was a " Hall of Fame" evening because there were only tickets for two to that event, but I remember being seated at a table with Gilda Radnor, Lorraine Newman and Walter Cronkite and his wife. Since I was now a diehard "Saturday Night Live" fan, I wanted to talk to the "girls." But Mrs. Cronkite, who was a fan of Dad's and a really nice woman, said those familiar words over and over: "I'd like you to meet my son." It's so funny to think about now. I never gave a number or got a call. I just figured those things work themselves out. Her son probably heard "I met a nice girl for you," too. *Que sera sera.*

Chapter Fifteen

Now I had spent my first year away at school at Stony Brook, and it became apparent that this was never going to work. It was just too expensive and hard. I was making straight A's, but no one was really interested. I wrote a paper in my English class about what growing up backstage meant to me. It was titled "The Night." The professor made 30 copies and handed it out to the students as an example of what she was looking for in her final paper. I don't have a copy. Everyone in class had to repeat the assignment except for me. It felt wonderful. I fell in love with writing and thought about turning that assignment into a book even back then. But I was only 20 at the time, not enough experience yet.

Every weekend I would drive back home to work, and have a nice Saturday date night. Dad was mostly booked for concerts on weekends and had started the Nassau Community Folk Festival. His good friend Harry Chapin, whose home was on Long Island, and who filled in for Dad anytime someone didn't show or cancelled last minute, was such a lovely man. My father knew him from back in the Canada Days of "Let's Sing Out," when he performed with his brothers. Harry never forgot the favor, and they became good friends. Dinner at Harry's place was hectic; I think he had five children, but with my brothers there and probably lots of friends, it seemed like more.

It was a warm hospitable place. I loved it. It's the way I hoped our house could have been. But I believe it was too unstructured for my young stepmother, who really never looked comfortable at these parties. Always dressed up and above it all, regal in a way that was at odds with the folk music dynamic. Although I'm sure she loved being part of it, she nevertheless seemed to me to be an outsider.

My father once told me a story, which I think he repeated at the tribute concert when Harry Chapin died. He met Harry by accident on a plane going somewhere; they sat together and talked about family and how travel really took its toll. Later that year Harry Chapin had his breakout hit "Cat's in the Cradle." Then rushing to a benefit, as we all know, Harry Chapin died in a horrific accident on the Long Island Expressway. My father always added that song to his play list after that, as a tribute to his friend.

When my employers read in the paper about the "Tribute" to Harry, which also had a picture of my father, I think they finally got whose daughter I was. Up until then, it was just part of the resume of my life.

People are funny when they realize my father has a name they ought to recognize. Sometimes they ask a few questions, and I might relay a song they might know, depending on their age, or a television show, mostly *Sesame Street* gets a reaction. On this occasion, the newspaper coverage earned me a different kind of respect, always a bonus when working for someone. Top salesgirl and a famous father, somehow the two always connected.

By this time, I intended to transfer to Nassau Community College, because I could afford it, and I assumed I would finish up back at Stonybrook, after saving some money. It was the Spring of 1976 and suddenly Dad was in demand again. My father had completely reinvented himself by writing a book, called *The Spirit of '76*. This book was not only perfect timing for our Bicentennial, but was also available on cassette tapes for schools. It showcased the Revolution from both sides of the war and was an immediate bestseller.

Partially as a result of this, Dad had an engagement to sing at the unveiling of the original Star Spangled Banner at the Smithsonian Museum and a show at the Kennedy Center. The show starred his old friend from Broadway, John Raitt, along with Jean Ritchie and her sons, Jay and Molly Ungar, and others. There was much excitement about all of this and I got a call that I must drive down immediately to Washington, D.C. with a trunk load of books, because they were selling out at every performance. Not to worry, arrangements had been made for me: just take 95 south and get off at the Washington Beltway.

Those were my instructions. Period. I live in Washington, D. C. now, so those of you who are guessing what happened are laughing already; but I assure you, by the third trip around the Beltway, and eleven hours later, things starting to look familiar; it wasn't funny. I finally arrived at the grand Embassy Suites Hotel, where a party was going on, and dropped off the books. Exhausted, all I wanted was a room key, but I was informed by my stepmother that these suites were for long term guests and she had found a nice hotel for the night for me across town.

So that's where I went. Was I livid? Yes. Did I feel completely underappreciated? Yes. Would I have liked to join the festivities? Yes. The Jefferson Hotel, a national landmark, but not a luxury hotel. Did I say anything? No, so no one knew how I felt as usual, and no one can be blamed. *Can't act on information I don't have.* That was my father's favorite saying. So next day I went to the show and drove home.

Now I had a big decision to make. Although at the time, I didn't know that I was even making one. Jean's family had a tradition of spending a few weeks in Kentucky, in the summer, at a family reunion. They had a very old, friendly dog, named Freddy. He was too old to make the trip that year, so Jean and George asked if I would stay in the house and take care of Freddy. This was a great idea. I loved the house, the dog, and the thought of some summer independence.

By that time, I had moved on to a better and higher class of jewelry store on the Miracle Mile in Manhasset, so this was perfect. Just one town away.

Now remember the lovely young man I was seeing? The one who took me to SNL? Well, he had a plan to go to Europe that summer with his best buddy; this seemed to be really working out for everyone. However, at the last minute his buddy fell in love and my guy ended up travelling regretting his decision not to ask me to go with him. Probably, another time that the stars realigned and changed my life. I had a great summer, I remember sleeping in the big bed downstairs because the dog couldn't make it upstairs. Jean and George never locked their front door, so I would tie a leash from the doorknob to the kitchen chair at night. Great security, but the house was set so far back in the woods, that only kinfolk and friends would know it was there, and besides I had an old dog to protect me. Sadly, even though I took great care of him, upon the return of the family, Freddy passed away. I truly believe he was just waiting for them to come home.

By the time my friend came back from Europe, it was clear that friendship – rather than continued romance – was in the cards. So we made a pact to throw a great party; I would invite some single girls and he would have his buddies over.

Great idea, a party at the Brand house was always a success. First of all because I recognized early that food was really important; no chips and dip for my parties. Full on bakery and spread. More importantly, the music room, or "Blue Room" where Dad had all his recording equipment and instruments, was never off limits. And because every young man at that age fancied himself a rock star, they enjoyed the jamming and fooling around with the guitars and drum set.

Dad only had one rule. No smoking dope. I know it's correct to call it weed now, but we called it dope, and it was forbidden. The explanation was that if I got arrested, it would be Dad's reputation that would be hurt. So I put a sign on the door that said: "If you must get small, please get small outside." It was a reference to Steve Martin's first comedy album. Nobody seemed to mind the restriction, since the food and music was great, and I learned a very important lesson about peer pressure. It doesn't really exist, unless you let it.

It was at this party that I met my next boyfriend. On and off for four years. He was the funniest, wittiest person I had ever met. Just the quick comebacks and intellectual dueling made me fall hard, but cautiously. He also had what I considered a mean streak, but was probably just immaturity in retrospect.

Because this relationship was volatile from the start, breakups and brokenhearted separations lasted sometimes for a while. In between one of the breakups, I met a handsome, bearded medical student who was older and seemed to have the same type of gentle demeanor as my Dad. He was studying to be a psychiatrist, just perfect, and was calmly analyzing everything I would do or say. I didn't mind that, maybe I liked it. I know I fell for him.

My father, who studied Freud in College, always said that a girl looks for her father in all men. Maybe not appropriate to hear, but definitely a stamp of approval for the soon to be doctor. I was 21 years old, in love, ready to leap into domesticity, which I had basically been preparing for my whole life, so when he proposed marriage, with the blessing of his mother and his grandmother's engagement ring, I said yes. You would think someone might have suggested I was too young. Maybe my stepmother or father?

But in a way, with all the responsibility, this looked good on paper and we celebrated with a lovely party. I mean the pedigree was there and my future was stable, so why not?

Here's your answer, a few days after graduation from medical school, he broke off the engagement citing it was too soon and I was too young. He was right of course and there is a syndrome I have heard of which is all too common among medical school graduates. They know you have seen them suffer at their worst moments, their first corpse or first death. Now they are officially doctors and big shot interns. You are yesterday's news. I returned the ring, because it was the right thing to do, but was completely distraught emotionally.

I was clearly coming apart, rejection just wasn't part of my vocabulary, so I went to my father for advice, and his answer was to go to Europe. Take a vacation to Paris! He told me I would never see Europe the same way again, as a young person. I found my childhood friend from Croton who was willing and had the money, plus she was meeting her grandmother there in a few weeks for an extended trip to Germany. This is what I needed, space, adventure and time to mend my broken heart. I took an extended leave from work and off we went.

What an adventure, what a great plan! Two young girls alone in Paris, France. What could possibly go wrong? The gardens were gorgeous, the hotel, large, safe and in the middle of everything, walking distance to the Patisserie. So we checked in, booked a tour for the next day and visited the Louvre.

On the walk back to the hotel the first day, without provocation, a man grabbed me and smashed me against the wall of a building, mashing my breasts and trying to kiss me.

A total stranger, an ambulance driver heard my friend screaming for help, jumped out of his vehicle and pulled the man off me. Then he punched him in the face and the man went down. I will never forget that sound, because it didn't sound like television or the movies, it sounded like meat being slapped.

We were so grateful to our hero, and thanked him profusely, even asking to take a photograph of him so I could tell the story later with a picture to prove it happened. Oh, we were so very naïve, to think this would just be a story for our little vacation. I did not feel in the least bit violated, I felt annoyed and angry, but I knew I hadn't done anything except walk down the street, so again, not my fault. Lots of hugging and Oui, Oui, Merci, and he was on his way.

We were excited about our tour the next day, so we went back to the hotel to sleep. This would be the last night we would spend together as friends.

Chapter Sixteen

The following morning we boarded a bus for a tour of the city, which would end in a delicious dinner and then the city lit up at night. I dressed casually in jean skirt and tee shirt with a cute little silk scarf from the flea market we had found the day before. My friend, was also casual, a great deal shorter and plumper than I, but adorable with a wonderful smile. We were so amused by our handsome tour guide, who spoke French, but discovered that he was a student from England, just there for the summer job. This was a great relief to everyone on the bus, because few, if anyone, actually spoke French.

Giles, I will never forget that name, had a delightful repore with everybody and was very flirtatious. I am sure this might have been frowned upon elsewhere, but we were in France, so all the nice ladies on the bus enjoyed it, and my friend especially thought his flirting was directed at her. He was handsome, charming, and exotic. So when dinner was over we stopped at a Patisserie for sweets and he suggested walking us inside the hotel. My friend was thrilled, thinking he was interested in her, but when he turned his attention to me, she stormed off to walk the halls until my "date" was over. I would have done the same for her, without the anger.

We took all the goodies up to my room and I turned my back to close the door and felt his hands on my neck. I was thrown onto the bed, literally attacked from behind while being choked, and thinking the best way out of this was not to fight. This was date-rape before anyone ever had spoken those words. But I didn't know any better than to go along or die. In about five minutes, he was gone. I heard him cursing Americans and women in general, but I didn't care, I just broke down crying. By the time my friend returned, I was still pretty hysterical and she was still angry and not buying any of it. She said she was leaving to meet her grandmother early and had already made the arrangements. We went to sleep and by the next morning she could see the bruises on my neck, but she still chose to go. I was on my own again. So what does a girl do?

Well, first I had nine more days to pass, so I started walking the streets collecting food. I have no idea why, but I spread all this food on my bed, yes the same bed, and stuffed my face. I felt a little better. Then I went to the museums, better. Another day a trip to Chartres. The little town and church, ancient and lovely, better still. Next Montmartre, where all the great artists I had read about exhibited their work. Much better still. Ok one day at a time in a beautiful city and then home.

First of all, I wasn't the broken-hearted girl that had arrived just a week earlier. Secondly, I kept repeating the lesson my father told me, that it wasn't my fault. So I decided right then and there, what happened in Paris, would stay in Paris. No one ever knew.

There is discord here, because of all the things that have happened to me, this is the story my family would like me to leave out. They feel it will somehow reflect badly on them. After over 40 years, my stepmother asked me why I never said anything, but also she added that she guessed I dealt with it because I seem okay. I probably could have used professional help back then, but this next paragraph will tell you why I didn't ask.

By the time I came home, my step-mother's father was quite ill. He passed away very quickly and it wasn't a time to burden anyone with my problems. Then unfortunately, soon after, her mother became ill. Just terrible for anyone who was as close as she was to her mother. A decision was made that she and my father would help in her mother's care by spending as much time in Philadelphia as possible, which left my brother James in my care. No one asked. I was still working, but homework needed explaining and bullies were surrounding this odd kid with the vivid imagination, but not a great attention span. So I just did what I always did. I helped out.

The good news was that for a while recovery seemed probable

and the folks would be returning soon. I made peace with my ex-boyfriend, and we were on again. I still kept in touch with a couple of prospects from high school, because I never really trusted that this relationship would last. I wasn't a serial dater, and I wasn't cheating on anyone, I just felt this was an opportunity not to make any more mistakes. I wanted a nice safe guy. I was going to be 22 and felt like I had lived a lifetime already. Time for Jeannie to have some fun. I attended the Yale Prom, a great tradition of girls on the train with long dresses, to be met by their fellows in New Haven for a long weekend of classy parties and dances. I visited my old beau from New York at Harvard and we had a wonderful time. Later he told me that he had met someone, but nothing serious yet. I get it, you really can't count on junior high through college to work out, but they ended up getting married, and I always regretted not being a better girlfriend, because he was really a decent fellow, and I probably would have been better off with him. But there are no regrets. I was pushing back against so much responsibility, and no one was aware of the mountain of stress I shouldered.

It was a time when people were having fun, before settling down. I turned back to the guy who was entertaining. One dimensional maybe, nothing under the surface, definitely. The guy you rely on for a good joke, a good time, a good adventure. Emotional support was not his strong point.

One thing I will say about this young man, is that he got it. He saw firsthand how absurd my situation at home was. I liked his family, he had a great mother, funny how that thread is always woven into my thoughts. Almost every single person I dated, had either lost their father, or had a very strong mother, who liked me. I was always searching, but I wasn't aware of it at the time.

This opened another chapter in my life that is really surprising. I had a dream that I saw my maternal grandmother, and in the dream, her face was a gorilla's. Little pieces of its face fell away bit by bit, to reveal my grandmother. Wow! I went right to dad with this one. He very generously liked to hear dreams and analyze them, Freudian that he was.

His conclusion was that I was afraid of her because I didn't know her. He thought I should get in touch with her. She still lived in the Village and was a painter. Sounded pretty cool. I looked her up, and we became family instantly again, with only one rule. Neither one of us could mention my mother. She had her reasons, a ridiculous lawsuit over my grandfather's estate, and of course I had all of mine. Her apartment was devoid of any photographs of family and except for all the paintings that she had painted at the Art Students League. A one room apartment with a tiny efficiency kitchen and bathroom. She had a tiny parakeet named *Chotkie* that had flown into her window one day, and never left.

It just sat on her shoulder all the time, unless she was out. There was one bed and a great view from the top floor of West Houston Street, looking north up Sixth Ave. A sunny view with tiny violets in pots in every window. I had a bohemian grandma!

Since she blamed my father for my mother's drinking, all those parties they hosted, we didn't speak of him either. To be fair, he was instrumental in our reunion, but of course, she didn't see it that way. Grandma knew I would return to her someday and that's what kept her going. My brothers didn't seem to interest her much, maybe too painful a reminder of all that she had lost. So we mostly talked about me , and that was a nice change.

Her feeling of being an outsider and an orphan followed her for all her life. I always think of the piece of cheese and bread she would bring from the senior center, in her bag, for dinner. Or the one strawberry, added to Knox gelatin for a special treat.

I ate it because I knew it was special to her and I thought she was so careful with her money, but when she passed away, she had $600,000 in her account. I'm not even sure she was aware. Hence, the lawyers and accusations.

The funny thing is that I would take a train all the way to the city to see her, lay down on her bed and promptly fall asleep. I guess I just felt so relaxed there. All she wanted was to make me comfortable and expected nothing in return. How delightful and refreshing.

She introduced me to some family on my mother's side, but they were predisposed not to like or trust me because mostly everyone had been taken advantage of by my mother at some point. Apparently, my great uncle, who had invented a cooling system for canned shrimp and sold this process to Bumble Bee, was the target of one of my mother's suits. So, I was an outsider and never felt really included, although I met some second cousins that were close to my age and later became friendly with them. My great uncle was actually not my grandmother's brother, but her nephew, born of the older sister who rescued her. But as they had grown up together as children, he became very much like a brother and, later, protector and business manager. He took good care of her and her assets, and she profited from it. My grandmother wasn't poor. Still, she may have been unaware or just did not care. As long as her bills were paid, she was happy.

I only had a few years with her. She didn't come to my wedding, because I was married in my father's house, but she was there in spirit and approved. I learned some things about my heritage and her tragic childhood. Also a little about my grandfather, who she said had come from a rich family – though they disowned him when he married her, since she had no family or pedigree.

The real tragedy of divorce is always the collateral damage to grandparents. She missed out on a lot. So did I. A few year later, when she felt poorly, she decided to walk herself to St. Vincent's Hospital, where she had a heart attack on the way and died alone. Rumor was that she had a new will in her pocketbook that day and it named her three grandchildren in it, but that just caused more lawsuits and speculation.

I didn't attend her funeral, I knew who would be there. Everyone forgave me, there was the graveside scene that I fully expected and knew in advance would happen, so I stayed home and prayed she'd understand. I'm sure she did.

Chapter Seventeen

By 1978, I had racked up plenty of college credits and found myself writing for a literary quarterly called "Fragments" magazine. The joke being that we only had the money to publish twice a year. My brother Eric went to Stony Brook, straight out of high school, because he took out loans and dad had the money then. Good for him. He graduated and became a T.V. writer in California for HBO, "Grace Under Fire" and "Cosby." He also became an Orthodox Jew, explaining that he had researched all religions and found he liked this one best, plus he finally felt like he belonged to a huge extended family. I respect that and understood. He married his sweetheart, and he actually had a bar mitzvah at 30 years old. Never a hypocrite and very self-assured, he managed to fit this lifestyle into living in Hollywood for a while, but came back to New York eventually and to the banking industry.

I was living at home when the big announcement came that there would be another addition to the Brand family. I can tell you now that I was expecting that it would happen, but my younger brother James, who only wanted a mommy to guide and protect him, was completely blindsided. Yes, we made a big fuss and were very excited. I was sure this would cement the family and we would never have to worry about moving again, and I was correct. My father was 58 years old when my youngest brother was born. With the advantages of money, my brother Jordan, had everything he needed, at the moment he needed it.

My brother James was in shock. I came up with an idea for James that he still credits to this day for setting him on the right path. I gave him a magic set. That may seem like a small token, but with such low self-esteem already, the painted face as a clown and the remarkable ability to entertain, became his life's work. Eventually, he traded in the costume for a more mystical approach, changed his name to James Brandon, and travelled the world, gaining mass applause, which helped him become whole again. Bravo for him. (On one occasion, before fame hit, James's friend David Copperfield asked him if I would be interested in a date. I wasn't impressed by his approach and turned him down. Path not taken.) My brother eventually married a supermodel and had two fine boys. He still calls me every day, to make sure I am okay, and of course there is no doubt that I consider him my firstborn.

Jeannie, 22 years old, with brother Jordan. (Brand Family Collection.)

My step-mother's mother lived to see her grandson, but sadly died soon after. Every bit of love that was available was poured into our little brother, literally from the day he was born. And the household changed again.

Separation of money now was obvious, with food literally labeled in the refrigerator for only his consumption. Toys littered the house. And every accommodation to his needs met, without regard for bedtime or boundaries. Psychologically, living under these conditions, while working and going to school, became impossible.

You may find this hard to believe, but there was never any jealousy or bad feelings towards our newest sibling. Most of the resentment was directed at our parents, who truly didn't see the inequities of how we were being treated. At 22 years old, I saw the future.

So since this is my book, and I am a kind person, I will just say that given all the benefits of having money, doesn't compensate for close personal relationships. I was determined to have this with my new brother, never differentiating him from my other brothers. I made sure to play with him, cuddle him, and help as much as I could. But eventually, the writing on the wall was clear. Time to move out. Karen came to me upset that my father didn't want me to leave, but it was my decision. I thought it was right for the family.

Besides, I was moving into Jean Ritchie's basement apartment. Not across the country. Still free to babysit and be a big sister. The day I moved out, my father cancelled my car insurance. The only thing he ever helped me pay for. On your own is on your own.

Jean and George were welcoming and wonderful. They waited up for me when I came home from a date. They wanted to hear all about it. Jean had her "girl." Her son Jon had opened up a Café in town. He was an excellent cook, but this café also boasted a weekly performance, sometimes by a local singer, or family and sometimes, with his connections, someone really famous. The food was great and the atmosphere warm and welcoming. I was really happy and felt at home. When Dolly Parton had her T.V. show and she sang Jean's song "Dear Companion" we all gathered around the T.V. set together.

I was now relaxed and enjoying the company of my funny valentine – unfortunately, the best friend of my former boyfriend.

But we now know how that happened. I was working by day and still trying to complete my degree. Jean was so good to me and of course I was always welcomed upstairs; but she also charged me rent, because how else was I supposed to learn. I understood that, no hard feelings there. The Brands continued to have all their holidays with the Pickows – so on on those days all I had to do was walk up the stairs to see my family.

I finally got a great trip to Europe with my boyfriend. He was really an adventure seeker, and that summer, Freddie Laker opened up round trip air fare from the U.S. to Amsterdam for $149. It was a fantastic marketing idea. The only flaw was that you purchased a ticket in the U. S. for $100 and then in Amsterdam, another ticket to come home for $49. What could possibly go wrong?

Well for one thing, anybody that wanted to come to America could now do so for under $50! So by the time we were done with our adventure of sleeping on trains and visiting every European country we could think of until our money ran out, the trip home became a free for all at the airport.

The Palace at Versailles had just been bombed, so soldiers our age were strutting around the airport with machine guns. This wasn't fun anymore. Worse, they decided a lottery system was the only fair way to get us home, so I spent three days in the ladies room hiding and waiting for my number to come up. This is absolutely true. My boyfriend actually gave up his seat because he was the last number called, and I would have had to stay behind. I thought it was so romantic, but I realize in retrospect that he could have given it up to me!

After we returned to the States, I started to get a little restless. I was reexamining my relationship, wondering if I really came first, plus this guy had a history of using recreational drugs, and yes, I was a prude when it came to these things. I was afraid because of the terrible experiences with my mother, I decided I needed a change.

I took a summer job in Southampton, NY where a cousin had offered a beach house and small wages in exchange for rubbing elbows with the rich and famous and selling antique quilts. The decision to do this changed my life forever.

As soon as I started to work, I met all sorts of interesting people. There was a great divide betwen the "Townies" and the "Summer" people. The Townies worked and lived in Southampton all year long. The "Summer" people had their mansions and summer homes there, but mostly came out on weekends. Or vacationed there all summer if they were from "old money." I did very well for my cousin. Noticing that during the sunny days, people were at the beach, I started opening at night for the after dinner strollers.

One day Gloria Vanderbilt came in. I pretended not to know who she was, but recognized her from her blue jean campaign. She ended up purchasing 13 quilts from me. It was a record sale. I found out later that she used them in an entrance hall covered in lacquer. Not what antique quilts were meant for, but out of my hands.

I sold to Faye Dunaway, and a few more celebrities. Meanwhile, thanks to the separation, my boyfriend missed me enough to want to marry me.

Great, now I was an engaged gal, on the hottest property in New York, and strangely, not terribly excited about it. Maybe because my fiancé told me to make my own ring and he'd pay for it, or maybe because when I'd say "I love you" he'd say "ditto." It just wasn't clicking.

One sunny day, I was sitting on the wicker porch swing that hung from the middle of the ceiling in the quilt shop, sewing the damaged old quilts to pass the time and listening to the radio. A lady walked in with a gentleman, casually dressed, but wearing jewelry that I noticed immediately to be antique and unusual. We began a pleasant conversation, and after a while they made themselves comfortable on the settee in the corner. The woman had a wide smile and a hearty laugh, we were getting on great and really having a delightful conversation. I'm not sure how long they were there, maybe an hour or more, but the lady said, "I have a son, I would like you to meet." I had heard this so often, that we all had a good laugh over it.

The gentlemen by her side was her brother, and he was in the antique business too. He was also a good deal younger and was a fan of my father's and folk music in general. All of which I found out later. At that time, I think I was just falling in love with this woman who looked nothing like me, but thought exactly as I did.

From that first day, we forged more than a friendship, and later that day, when she brought her very shy son along with other family members for cover, I had the guts to say to him: "Come back later, at closing time, without your family."

I know this wasn't cool, because I was engaged. But I still didn't have a ring. What I had was lots of doubts. And this gorgeous, shy, Olympic athlete seemed very enticing. So he brought me over to the house to meet the rest of the family. I guess it was a first date. I just talked and talked with his mother, while his father sat and stared at me from his comfortable chair. They had an eclectic beach house, off the beaten path and such a welcoming, fun attitude. We even rolled back the carpet and danced to some 45s! I felt like I was in a dream.

The young man, named *Jim*, was so shy, he barely said a word, except that he had just graduated from Georgetown University and was taking time off after a grueling tour of running for the University on a full athletic scholarship. This was like speaking a different language to me. I hadn't known many athletes, maybe none in fact. But I knew a good, straight, kind man when I saw one. He let it slip that he had already scoped me out through the window of the store with his friends; he assumed I had a boyfriend, and was not surprised when I told him that I was sort of engaged. I promised to go home and break it off, and I did.

There was plenty of drama and confusion after that. My father was clear. He said: "Don't marry either of them. You're basically coming out of a divorce and the other is a rebound." But George and Jean sat me down and had a real heart to heart with me. George told me there were no guarantees in life and I should go with my heart. Jean said the same and confided that they'd had their differences, being of completely different backgrounds and religions. But as long as there was respect and love, it would be okay. That was a huge endorsement and I went with it. We've been married 34 years.

So now we come to my tiny wedding, quickly put together in three weeks, because we didn't want to offend anyone and live together first.

Married, 1982. (Brand Family Collection.)

One thing I will never forget about that wedding. As I walked down the tiny "aisle" in my father's living room, ready to meet my groom six feet away, Dad surprising me with an unrehearsed whisper in my ear. First he said: "hold" – the director in him, to pause for effect. Then he said: "Never think it will be easier with someone else." Nice. Two seconds to the ceremony and his best advice now? I guess he would know. He was on his third marriage by then, but what timing! I had asked for his advice months earlier, he just chose that moment to give it.

We have great video of that day. Jean mugging for the camera. Family. Friends. My father trying to give a toast to his only daughter and choking on the words. But by far the funniest moment, picked up by the microphone, is when Dad saw the spread on the table and – fearing there wouldn't be enough for everyone – gave the command: "Family, hold back."

Later in the day, my adorable and by now shirtless four year old brother had had enough of all the traditional protocol. So when the wedding cake was served, he said "I want a very, very, big piece!" We hadn't cut it yet, or done the ceremonial feeding each other, but fair is fair, and being a kid trumps being a bride or groom. Understood. And here's the irony. I had left the cake and arrangements to my stepmother. The beautiful white cake wound up being chocolate inside, which I am allergic too. But my father loved it and so did my little brother – so no harm, no foul. I just smiled and didn't swallow.

My mother-in-law was my biggest supporter. How many people can say that? We enjoyed every summer together, either antiquing in Southampton, or on her frequent visits to Washington, D.C. where Jim and I eventually landed and I opened up an antique shop, called "Three Wishes." Clever eh? A play on my name. After years of trying, Jim and I eventually adopted a Hungarian born son. (Story to come later.) This delighted his family, because my mother-in-law was full blooded Hungarian. Right from the beginning, he looked just like his Uncle John, my mother-in-law's brother. From the moment I met her she became *mom* to me, so that's how I will refer to her from now on. I think that she enjoyed my shop so much that eventually she opened her own, in upstate New York. Forever in my heart, and forever grateful for finally getting a taste of what a mother's love is like. Not always pretty, but real and always on your side. No matter what.

I can hear her voice in my ear whenever I see people who weren't up to her standards. She had a regal bearing and excellent taste. She taught me all about the provenance of an item. Never at a loss for words, we chatted daily on the phone about customers. She was always thrilled when I made a sale and loved my stories. She passed away a few years ago, and at her funeral I told the story of how I met my husband. I like to say she picked me out for him. I now have a huge extended family, including 24 nieces and nephews.

Move to D.C. - Three days after wedding, 1982. Jean Ritchie's house in background. (Brand Family Collection.)

On our first anniversary, we travelled to New York, to celebrate in Southampton and revisit the store where we met, maybe see the fireworks on July 4th. It was a lovely day. We had borrowed my stepmother's car because we had flown up for the long weekend. I had an idea to beat the traffic home and to leave early that night. As we drove along the familiar Long Island Expressway, Jim felt the tire go flat. He got out and changed it.

Then a few miles later, another sound, under the hood, like leaking steam. Sure enough, a leaking hose. Being resourceful, we pulled into a rest stop and literally peeled the plastic sign off a coke machine to use as tape. We proceeded home at about 30 miles per hour. We knew that AAA would be busy on July 4th and just wanted to get back safely.

While waiting at a light barely one mile from home, a car rushed passed us on the left. I have no memory of this. Then, I'm told, a police car in hot pursuit came crashing into the rear of our car! Fortunately, cars were tanks in those days. The entire back end was pushed into the seats we were sitting in. I was buckled in and my door was jammed shut. All I can recall is the hospital lights flashing above my head. Jim came away uninjured. He says I kept repeating "It's my stepmother's car" over and over. I was in shock, and was told later that I was suffering from hysterical amnesia and would eventually remember. I never did. All I know about that night is that my father had an appearance on the Today Show. The limo was waiting outside his house early that morning; and he was waiting to see if I would die, before he would cancel his appearance. Jim called to say that I had some internal injuries but that eventually I'd be okay, so away he went. The show must go on.

I never regained my memory of that night, but I know that July 4th remains my least favorite holiday. These days I stay home and watch the fireworks on television with the sound off. Some aspects of the psychological trauma persist to this day; it would be a year until I could sit in the passenger seat again.

Jim and I travelled for a few years with my father, Karen, and Jordan, when he was still very young, on ski vacations and summer adventures. We were a little substitute sibling family. My other brothers had already left the house by then and it was very important at the time for Jordan to have this relationship. Jim was like a big brother to Jordan, and I got to spend some really wonderful quality time with my young brother. I knew he needed the sibling experience, so even in my thirties, I was playing games and putting on plays for the parents. But after he was sent to boarding school, the visits became less frequent.

I have met many people since then who didn't know that my father had any children other than Jordan. I have been introduced at social gatherings, and have more than once seen looks of surprise on people's faces. It's one of the reasons I am writing this book. The other is that I am determined to keep my father's legacy alive the way I believe he would want it. With all his children included.

Chapter Eighteen

When my husband and I first moved to Washington, D.C. in 1982, we used to listen to a radio program called *Music Americana,* hosted by Dick Cerri. There was no internet then, so I couldn't stream Dad's WNYC show. Cerri's was the next best thing. One day Dick had a contest, and I decided to write into the station. Yes, I mentioned I was Oscar Brand's daughter, with the suggestion that he play more of my father on his show. Dick was such a gentlemen. I got a letter back inviting my father to appear at one of the showcases he hosted. This was serendipity, because except for the weekly appearance on NPR, when we would sometimes meet for dinner later, I rarely saw Dad perform. I used to fly back "home" a lot back then, but these trips took place mostly when I was needed to babysit Jordan. Nice to know I was so trusted.

One time, we were driving Dad to the plane, instead of a train, because he was in a hurry. The traffic was awful. We were so close to the airport that planes were flying low right over our heads. My father, never one to be late or miss a performance, jumped out of the car and ran across the highway, guitar case on his back. Rest assured that he made the plane. Can you imagine anything like that taking place now? It reminded me immediately of the same circumstances that happened years before, when we had added air conditioning to our little Comet two-door sedan. (My birth-mother was with us and there was only one brother, Eric, so this is a really early memory.) We were taking Dad to the airport from Manhattan. The car overheated in the Lincoln Tunnel. Dad got out of the car and hitched a ride to the airport, to make his plane and his concert on time. We were left waiting for a tow truck. Again, no cellphones, and probably a deal breaker moment in their marriage. Of course, that's just speculation. All marriages have those moments, and then you go on, or you don't. Period.

Since I loved to have my father visit me and as a new bride, I arranged many gigs near my home in Washington, usually to coincide with a big Folk Festival, but sometimes just a few libraries or small venues.

When Dad appeared at the Washington Hilton, I had a taste again of what my old life had been and I was homesick. We had moved to Washington, D.C. specifically so my husband could train with his old coach at Georgetown for the 1984 Olympics. He had a couple of inconsequential jobs that allowed him to leave early to train, while I worked at a busy downtown jewelry store, then took the unfinished Metro and bus home to Connecticut Heights and our lovely little one bedroom apartment. Then Jim stepped on a severed signpost and injured his heel, and the Olympic dream faded. Now there was nothing really keeping us there and when the call came from Wallach Sons of Manhasset, to come back at double my previous salary, it hardly took any convincing.

I had worked with the Wallach family for so many years. I babysat their grandchildren, and of course, they were in just about every photo from my wedding. I was delighted to be back with them and back on the Miracle Mile, close to home base, Jean and family, the folks and my new in-laws, whose company I truly adored. We moved into a carriage house on the old Whitney Estate, decorated by my mother-in-law and new favorite uncles. Jim's uncles were eight and ten years older, unmarried, talented antique dealers and my new best friends.

I spent a lot of time at my parent's house less than a mile away, that's when we forged such a strong relationship with my youngest sibling, because now I was available for soccer games and field trips and babysitting all the time. We often ate at the folks to save money. Jim had a job in the city and things were going pretty well. Every weekend Dad had a concert and in the summer he performed at recreational parks outdoors. These were wonderful times.

If I wasn't working, the uncles and I would take off on hunting expeditions for the next great antique find; they didn't drive, so I was the ride, but they were great company. I would take my summer vacation in the Hamptons with my mother-in-law, the men joining us on the weekends. The two of us alone would giggle and sleep late. Then maybe a trip to the local thrift, which in Southampton is an anomaly, since everything in the store was high class. We'd eat giant shrimp on pumpernickel bread and watch old Woody Allen movies.

I think I might have been happy then, it seems that way as I write about it, but something was definitely going to interfere in this security blanket, I had finally found, I just didn't know how soon it would happen.

One day, just for the fun of it, I got a call from my mother-in-law that the house across the street was for sale. Hmmm, that sounded like a plan, let's go take a look. The house was in horrible condition, but it put the idea into our heads that maybe it was time to buy something. In those days all it took was a job to secure a condo at the least and a small down payment.

Guess what? An apartment became available right across the street from my in laws, we put up a check and had our first real home. The only problem for me was now I had a long commute from Westchester to Long Island. So one day, on my day off, I interviewed for a job at Neiman Marcus in their fine jewelry department. With my credentials, and easy natural ability to make a new best friend with the manager on the spot, I got the job. It didn't occur to me that the Wallach family felt that I had betrayed them in some way. I had a right to live my life, no promises were made, but there were hard feelings just the same. I regret that and think of them often with great affection.

Now I was the Bell of the Ball. Every dinner I held at the little apartment included wonderful food from the glamorous Epicure department at Neiman Marcus.

I was invited to all events that my father attended with Karen, so that Jordan would not be left at home. I didn't care, this was fun.

A favorite memory was the old Roseland Ballroom, with Elizabeth Taylor in attendance. As she left, she was surrounded by a huge entourage, but when she saw me playing with my little brother in the lobby, they parted and she came over to touch his curly head and smile.

She really did have violet eyes and obviously loved children. So with everyone clamoring for attention, I didn't even have to try. It was very sweet and another lasting memory for a lifetime.

Dad and Karen had joined an exclusive club on Manhasset Bay so that Jordan could swim and take tennis lessons. I sometimes watched on my day off. He was enrolled at Buckley Country Day School, where most of the prominent Long Island families sent their children. He was a wonderful student. Karen joined the board of directors; my father wrote the new school song. We attended their yearly school fair. Most of my Herend porcelain collection came from the school fair! My brother and I were very close; we made a button with our picture on it every year, and I still have them.

No jealousy whatsoever, I promise; this was a wonderful kid, full of love for his big sister and a pleasure to be with as long as we were alone. With the folks, there was always a watchful eye. I was trusted because I did things their way. I knew the rules.

The only problem, and it was a big one, was that my husband Jim had decided that it was time to start a family. I really wasn't keen on having children; frankly I was exhausted from all the childcare I had already done. But in any couple's life there is that discussion. I told Jim that at least I will think about it and get checked out to make sure the decision was mine to make, if and when I was ready.

My mother-in-law and I shopped for a beautiful hand-painted headboard, a vintage negligee, and in a crazy moment of full disclosure, a book of baby names. Most people wouldn't share these things with an in-law, but we weren't most people. And she was so excited at the prospect of grandchildren.

Chapter Nineteen

I remember mentioning a prescription for the pill, sometime way back in my teens, for endometriosis. Although no one used that term then, just a way to help out a girl with a problem that no one knew what to do about except prescribe opiate painkillers. The pill helped. I was on it for a long time.

By the time I did go off, it was obvious that something was terribly wrong. I had two miscarriages, before even consulting a specialist. There was no Google to look up the symptoms. Poor Jim had to be tested too, and go through excruciating surgeries, which I blame on his running days with no support garment, because it was uncomfortable. Come on, doesn't take a genius to figure out this might have an affect someday.

Now we were faced with what to do? As soon as this problem became apparent, we were thrust into another decision. Jim's job was offering an exciting transfer package to Washington, D.C. It was the chance of a lifetime; they would not only pay for moving and expenses, but an unheard of down payment on a house or condo. Could we resist? The answer of course was *no*, we couldn't. I really, really think it was a huge mistake, but the jewelry store in Washington wanted me back, no problem, and everyone promised to visit more often, so we moved.

Back to square one, but with an extra burden. I needed surgery first to fix a huge endometrial cyst and I liked the doctor in New York because for one thing he was the best and another he was a pioneer in the new in vitro fertilization technology, just in case.

We purchased a great apartment overlooking the Washington Cathedral, moved in, and decorated with the help of our dear Uncle John. Then, while Jim started his new job, I returned to New York for my surgery. What I didn't know was that everyone was afraid this giant baseball size "thing" on my uterus was cancer. No one spoke those words. My husband was in Washington, so my father sat by my bed in New York, reading the paper and holding my hand. The night before, a nurse came into the room and with great kindness sat on my bed and asked me if I was afraid. I was, so she gave me a little pill to help me sleep. I remember nothing after that except waking up to the news that there had been four cysts, more hiding behind the big one, and I didn't have cancer! My stepmother was there and my mother-in-law, and even the uncles. Everyone was so relieved. I never even knew this was a possibility, but if it had been, I had waited way too long to find out.

The doctor said in six months, fully healed, I could come back for the in vitro trials. I use the word "trials" because this was 1988. Now this is a very common procedure, but then it was completely experimental and my doctor was the only one doing it. Jim came up to New York for lessons on how to inject me with hormones. Right from the get go, I knew this was a bad idea. Maybe some couples have a tender touch, but he practiced on an orange, and I'm not an orange, so believe it or not I sent him packing for Washington, and stayed in my father's house while my stepmother gave me nightly injections for a month.

By then my brother was ten, interested in science, and already being groomed to be either a lawyer like his mother or a doctor like his grandfather. When the request came to watch my butt get an injection, purely for the learning experience, I really wasn't in a position to say *no*. After that the leap to actually giving his sister an injection was a given.

Before this even happened more than that one time, the popcorn feeling of exploding eggs started. I rushed to the hospital, Jim rushed to New York. I had nineteen eggs harvested, five fertilized and four developed. In those days, they didn't ask, all implanted. Then you wait. One test group got a bag with support hormones and one didn't. I remember distinctly asking for that bag and was told you have enough hormones to support a pregnancy, no bag. Hmmmmm, I think this was predetermined, but I waited the requisite nine days, and sure enough, all implanted, pregnant.

So, home to Washington, and special arrangements were made to Federal Express weekly blood samples to New York to follow my progress. Everyone was excited and delighted.

Jim had a business trip to California and was not home when I got a call that the levels were dropping and I needed to inject myself with the blessed support hormone. I sat there for hours. Just couldn't do it. I probably could have gone to an emergency room, but instead I knocked on the door of good neighbors. As it happened, they were having fertility problems too, and he was nice enough to oblige. So odd to think about now. Didn't matter. Nothing did. They were all gone, still in my body, but not "viable." Just a waiting game now. How awful to relive, and to think I was a test trial. The nurse on the phone told me "next" time I would get the hormones. I was still in "this" time.

My brother Eric came to stay with me. I vacuumed. I cleaned. We joked around a lot. Finally he had to go home. I was alone when I miscarried. I called my mother-in-law. I said, "I don't think I will ever be happy again." Her response was to get over it. Sound harsh? Yes, but exactly what I needed. I was alone and raging with emotion, she instinctively knew a cryfest was not in order.

By the time Jim returned, I was ready to go back to work. But something shifted again inside. Blame the hormones. Or blame our disconnection through the whole process. We were now on a downward spiral. I was not where I wanted to be. I felt horribly alone and depressed. I didn't think I could go through all that heartache again, but everyone at the hospital seemed to be pushing for another go. After all, for their purposes, I was a good outcome; no one as yet had a viable live birth, but I didn't know that at the time.

One day, on a visit to New York, I went to an exhibit at the Museum of Natural History to see the much revered Tiffany collection of jewelry. I was staring at the showcase for so long that I didn't notice someone staring at me from the other side. I looked up to find a dear friend of the family, whom I had run into the day before when I tagged along with my father for the opening of the, "Stardust" café – named for the beautiful and haunting classic song written by a good family friend, Mitchell Parish. Mitchell considered this man his "adopted" son. I might have mentioned the exhibit to this fellow, because here he was, just standing there looking at me.

Now I have already revealed that I have been married a very long time, so this is just a chapter in that marriage. But this is a memoir, which means every detail is not included, but the relevant ones must be.

This man seemed my partner in the way that is described in books and movies, but rarely found. Intellectually matched, sharp wit, a lover of Broadway and music, with an adoration for those people in the business. A little older and definitely connected to my world. I ate a wonderful sushi dinner with him, and met Mitchell Parish at his apartment, where misunderstanding the relationship, Mitchell gave his blessing not to let this one get away. Then onto the theatre for a Broadway show, and backstage to see Bill McCutcheon, who had been in "How to Steal an Election." He did a little dance for me when he found out I was Oscar's daughter. Such a sweet, delightful man.

Now I had to make a decision. New York and all it offered? Or go back to what remained of my marriage? I thought honesty was best, and I made the call that I needed to make. I said I needed a break, and to my surprise our entire apartment was quickly emptied and dispatched to storage. This was my mother-in-law's idea. Possession is nine tenths of the law and she wasn't letting go without a fight. It really wasn't Jim's idea, nor did either of us at that time think we were going to dissolve the marriage, but "mom" was making sure I knew who would be the big loser, and it wouldn't be her son.

Unfortunately, this was the catalyst for very hard feelings on both sides of the family that would take years to unravel. Now it was a turf war. I couldn't even reach Jim to talk; his mother wouldn't let us speak.

It was truly an outrageous predicament. So we waited. I stayed in New York and enjoyed going to the "Songwriter's Hall of Fame" induction ceremony, all dressed up and feeling very grand. My stepmother was actually very nice to me. My brothers and I secretly planned an anniversary surprise portrait for her, with all of us together at the sitting. The folks were going on another trip to Europe, so I was going to be alone in the big house. I felt unsure about everything and even asked my eleven year old brother, who seemed so wise, what he thought I should do about my marriage. Ahh, the mouths of babes. He said to do what I wanted, not what everyone expects. And off they went.

Hours later, Jim showed up at the door, making promises and pleading his case. I was lost. I always try to make everyone happy. This man was my husband. He was miserable. He seemed so sincere and so broken. So we reconciled. It wasn't as easy to convince the family, but we blamed it on the hormones. Good one. Probably true. That summer I was the bridesmaid for his only sister, so forgiven and happy in a pink Michael Kors gown, dancing at the Waldorf Astoria with my parents in attendance.

The one caveat was that we would have to move, I would never again feel happy in that apartment. So back to work, and treks with a real estate agent on weekends. It took only one week to realize that for the price of an apartment, we could afford a house in the suburbs.

On our first weekend we were exploring an area we already knew. We both loved it because of its close proximity to Rock Creek Park and the Howard Avenue Antique District. There we found it. A little Cape Cod, rented at the time, but with a 'for sale' sign on the lawn. Perfect for the family we now were determined to have together.

We had decided that was what was missing. Jim's sister was

already pregnant. Time to get on with it. I tossed out my bag of needles, and told everyone we knew that we wanted to adopt.

Jean Ritchie to the rescue again.

Karen and Oscar at Jordan's Bar Mitzfah.
(Brand Family Collection.)

Chapter Twenty

I'm not sure why everything in my life turns into a grand adventure, but this one sure did. The story of adopting our son was covered by newspapers, magazines and even a television interview, because it was part of a historic event which we were totally unaware of at the time.

From our perspective, it was a family affair. I knew I didn't want a domestic adoption because my best friend, Dana, had gone that route and there was too much open information available. Also, I figured that if I was going to put my time, energy, and love into raising my child, I didn't think another family coming to claim him later was for me. Open to dialog, but a better chance of it not happening if we weren't on the same continent. Sounds harsh, but actually I was wrong anyway, so here's how it went down. See if you can follow this tangled web.

My parents told their best friends, Jean and George, that we were adopting. George's sister had travelled a lot, and met and kept up a correspondence with a woman who was from Romania. That woman had a son, who was in medical school in Romania. The friend had recently passed away, but the son wanted to immigrate to America, so my stepmother who was an attorney, helped him with his paperwork and visa application. And there was our connection.

By the time we contacted the young doctor by mail, I had heard of all the terrible stories of the warehousing of children in state facilities. Also, the spread of AIDS had become rampant during the dictatorship of Nicolae Ceausescu, because his palace may have had $50,000 drapes, but his people were without food or basic supplies, so one needle was used to inoculate all the orphans. Many of the children had probably given up by loving parents who just couldn't support them and thought they were doing a brave and selfless act.

I looked up a local pediatrician, who told me the signs to look for when we went to Europe. Then we asked this young doctor to beg his aunt, the sister of our contact who had passed, to hold the baby in the hospital until we could get there. How was this possible? Well, it turns out that the aunt was the only doctor in a small town on the Hungarian border called *Oradea*. The position wielded a lot of power, and we were assured she would take care of this, as a repayment of the debt, the Americans held, by helping her nephew with his citizenship. Very complicated, but who cares, on our way, just a little paperwork with the INS, and of course, a healthy baby to adopt.

Now, if you think how we made this contact was complicated, just wait, we were so naïve. Americans have no idea until they see firsthand, what living under a dictatorship is like and how ordinary citizens turn to bribery and any means possible for food and work.

We had yet to actually identify the child, so I filled out paperwork ahead of time, leaving that part blank. Then off to the FBI for fingerprints and the Romanian Embassy on my lunch hour to get the visas in order.

Sometime in December we got a call that a Hungarian teenager had disgraced her family by becoming pregnant with a Romanian. This was unfortunate for her, because of the prejudices of her family, but a gift from God for us, because that meant our child would have the combined lineage of his parents-to-be. It was a sign. I was going to fight for this child.

Not so fast Jeannie. History intervened. On December 25th, 1989 the government was overthrown in a quick and unexpected civil war. The first family was taken to the town square and shot. The country was in a state of chaos. Did I know what that would mean to us? No, I was clueless, because it was not covered on our news, except as a Christmas story on the other side of the world, where small countries were going the way of the Soviet Union and Communism was failing. I was sure this would make everything easier.

All communication was cut off by then. But I remained determined not to let this adoption fail. An intermediary in Holland, could receive phone calls from Romania and then call us. At 2 A.M. on February 9, 1990, the phone rang.

Our son was born, healthy and ready. Photos were sent, which were strangely unsettling because they gave the first indication of how poor and unsophisticated the country was. The photos were black and white, smeared, and showed a naked child splayed out like an animal. The other was a photo of him swaddled tightly with a hand holding a large bottle. All I thought of was get there fast, this is one scary looking place, and I want my son home! That night I walked out onto our deck and stared at the full moon. John Denver's song "Shanghai Breezes" went through my mind. The lyrics that I sang to my little boy on the other side of the world were "It's the same old moon up in the sky."

We were told to bring money, of course, lipstick, size 10 and 12 women's clothing, lightbulbs, razors, and tons of diapers for the hospital. The other unsettling need was cigarettes, lots of them, which was the currency of the moment. So we did what we were told and got on that flight, which I jokingly call my 17 hours of labor, since I am deathly afraid to fly.

Three plane changes later and we were met at the airport by the doctor and a translator. Dr. D. as I refer to her, looked like my mother in law. Why not? She was full blooded Hungarian and as we had read on the plane in the newspapers covering the coup, the Hungarian nationals were not happy with the shifting politics and borders.

The Hungarians did not happily mix with the Romanians, and Oradea was a border town which had once been part of Hungary. For now, we were being led to the International Hotel, where food and lodging was available for Americans, but the Dr. and the interpreter would have to find other lodging. As the taxi drove through the streets, we could see the bullet holes in the buildings and the grey, polluted air. I can't remember if we were afraid. It was after the fact, but I knew nothing was in my control here and my lifelong talent of making friends was going to come in handy bigtime.

First day, we find out Matthew was still in the hospital waiting for us, and there is so much paperwork to do. That sounded like a good decision, visit the American Embassy, get his passport, and then fly to Oradea, which is basically the distance of New York to Virginia. Then pick him up and fly home. Did we know that we had arrived on Romania's version of Labor Day and all offices were closed? Or that the only thing we could do was go sightseeing at the looted palace? This is what Dr. D wanted, so we went. She held the keys.

That first night was scary because the chanting in the streets for the new government was in full display. I wanted to stay safe in the hotel. James wanted to explore. I was being ultra-careful, determined not to get sick. We had a water purifier with us that I used to wash with, and ate only bread and potatoes and fish for the entire time I was there. James ate whatever was served and immediately became ill. He had a cold and wore a mask because of the pollution. No one cared about us, except the masses outside the hotel, desperate to get in where there was at least some food.

The next day, closed or not, we managed to get the paperwork in front of the secretary of the new president. We just handed over anything we were told to. Can you imagine people from another country, coming to Washington, D.C. and going to the White House and asking that the president sign some adoption papers for you on your first day there? Would never happen unless you knew someone. That's when I understood how this was going to go, and how important this women was.

The Embassy told us our papers were in order. We were told to get the baby so they could sign off on the visa and we could make our plane home. There were no choices as far as time goes. There was just one flight available to us, or wait a month. So off we went to Oradea.

Oradea is a small town of about 250,000 people, 100,000 of them being Hungarian nationals. Dr. D was a big shot here. The only obstetrician who had delivered everyone's babies. After settling in at our "hotel" (basically an apartment building used for that purpose, with no amenities, which I expected, and infested with just about everything, which I did not), we were scheduled to go to the grave of the woman who had made this journey possible, Dr.D's sister. I wanted to meet my son so badly, but this was not my call. We went to the cemetery and stood over the grave to pray. I took the doctor's hand and held it. I believe to this day, that was the moment she was waiting for. The blood went through her veins into mine through our joined hands and I became family. No words necessary. Now back to her apartment for dinner.

I am not sure what I expected. Her being the only doctor in the town, I thought it might be grander, but it was a neat place, and remembering all the homeless people in Bucharest, the empty stores with no lights, gypsies selling peanuts in the doorways and on the sidewalks, this was definitely upscale.

I did not expect that when we entered the smoky apartment, we would be met by the mayor, the police captain, and assorted dignitaries who wanted to meet the Americans. I was seated in a big comfortable chair and little Matthew was brought out to be held, dressed in clothes we had sent ahead that morning, after learning the first batch had been stolen.

The room was a blur. I looked into his deep blue eyes. The connection was immediate. Moms always say that, but I swear everything else disappeared. We were in a bubble of bonding love. Then they had to practically rip him from my arms, as he was displayed on the dining table, to show his healthy body. There was a strange large coin covering his navel. I asked about it, but was told it was traditional. Later we found out that wasn't the case, but we're not there yet. He was taken away to the hospital for safe keeping. We had more work to do.

First time I held my son in Romania at "rendezvous" apartment. Interpreter looks on. April 29, 1990. (Brand Family Collection.)

The next morning was a blur of banks, notaries, officials and a new birth certificate, now with our names on it. This was all due to the connections of the good doctor. The afternoon was a different story. Everywhere we went, there seemed to be construction of some kind that had been either halted by the revolution, or begun and abandoned. I think the doctor wanted us to see the "old" Oradea. A place where people would come before the Cold War to rest and get the "cure." This was the famous "Fels Spa." During its heyday, 50 years before, this very luxurious resort had three pools where people would come from around the world to cure anything from arthritis to cancer. As we walked around the pools, we saw dead frogs and birds and exchanged knowing looks. The reason for their deaths were that these were natural uranium pools. No wonder they cured ills; they were the first radiation therapy.

The spa itself was so empty and devoid of life, but you could see by the grand furnishings that it used to be a haven and a lovely place to go for the cure. We nodded in approval. Big smiles all around and back to the apartment for dinner. I only add what might seem like a small detail because I distinctly noticed the centerpiece from the dining table was missing from the day before. It had been made of dried apples and wheat grasses. Spaghetti was served, because of course that's what Americans eat, and then desert: apple cake, freshly baked. The centerpiece.

The next morning we would pick up the baby and fly immediately back to Bucharest, where he had to be photographed and we'd get him a new passport. Fortunately, the interpreter was coming with us. We left all the clothes and amenities with the doctor as a sign of gratitude, and I gave her an amethyst birthstone ring to remember us by. With hugs and *visit us in America* salutations, we said our goodbyes. It would be less than a year before she took us up on the offer.

Next morning we were met at the hospital by the doctor and two nurses who wouldn't let us in. They would bring the baby out to us. The baby had been in hiding since birth because the law would have sent him to the orphanage after only three days, and the birthmother had left the country. There were other reasons, too. The place looked from the outside like a small trailer, no heat, lightbulbs, or running water.

I am sure they just didn't want us to see, and they were keeping a secret about the baby's health. Since I had requested no needles or inoculations, we had taken a big chance. But the little boy they handed me, along with two giant cans of powdered formula, looked fine to me.

We arrived at the tiny airport to see a plane straight out of the last take in the movie "Casablanca." Bald tires, propellers, and loaded with locals. Some money and cartons of cigarettes were exchanged, and three begrudged passengers were kicked off the plane to make room for us.

I had the baby in my lap. James sat in front of me, still sick. The interpreter, Monica, sat next to me. The trip across the Transylvanian Alps in a thunderstorm was harrowing. James reached back to hold my legs. I held the baby tightly, praying that we hadn't come this far only to be killed in a plane crash.

A flight attendant handed out some odd sucking candy for all the sickness going on. When we finally landed, I handed the baby to Monica, was first off the plane, and promptly threw up. So labor and morning sickness, check and check, not in order, but experienced.

Monica spent the night with us in the forbidden hotel. We needed her now. With two days to go, the Embassy threw every blockade in our way. There were other couples there who were having the same troubles. I will never know what happened to them, but when I said a new examination was impossible and translating all documents to English could not be done in time, the woman in the Embassy suggested in a very low voice that I must do it or risk the flight home, or worse, adopting at all. Who knew what new rules the government might put in place? She was right, although I didn't know at the time, that all adoptions were suspended just weeks after we left. And the new laws that were put into place required a six month waiting period.

So I left Monica to translate, and James to nurse his cold. I took the baby across town to a free clinic, which translates to *hell hole*, and bribed my way with cigarettes and lipstick to the head of the line. This place looked like an asylum, but it was on the approval list, so that's where I went. The doctor was a woman. I smiled. No smile back. Two cartons of cigarettes, of which she opened a pack and smoked one right in our faces while looking at the papers. She held the baby up by his head naked and examined his body over an open space heater. I watched and faithfully swore to heaven that no one would ever treat him without love and kindness while I drew breath.

Done. Raced to the hotel, grabbed everyone and the

paperwork. The Embassy took the requisite photos and looked over the paperwork, and a visa was issued. It was 4:52p.m. The Embassy closed at 5. Everyone cheered! We were going home.

With no communication to our parents, we had no idea that the 20/20 television programming, hosted by Barbara Walters and Hugh Downs, had just broken the story of the dreadful conditions in the Romanian orphanages. Our families were in a panic. They had no idea that we were not involved at all in this horror story. But somehow the media had caught on to our arrival and wanted our eyewitness account. It would have to wait; we were on a plane home.

Met at the gate and detained by officials, I wasn't giving this little package up for anything. We had placed an American flag in his carrier and were finally cleared, we walked through the gate into the loving arms of my mother-in-law, my sisters-in-law, and my father.

Dad was seventy when Matthew was born. As we followed him through the maze of cars at Kennedy Airport, I was thinking that this little boy must grow up knowing this amazing man. Not just through stories or books, but really know him. I wasn't sure how much time we'd have, but I was going to make it happen. What I couldn't possibly have known at the time was that they would celebrate their 20th and 90th birthdays together!

Jim was heading back to work in Washington, and I had an appointment the next day with a pediatrician, so I was staying in New York at Dad's and Karen's house.

My father-in-law stopped by the house to see the new baby. Jordan and my father took lots of photos. Then Karen and I decided a nice fresh bath would make everyone feel wonderful. I really needed help and sleep, it had been such a long journey running on adrenaline. I had left everything behind – all my clothes and even the suitcases with Monica because I knew she could barter them. I had nothing with me and we hadn't bought anything, being superstitious like most adoptive couples. So Karen and I dug through the basement and came up with Jordan's old bathtub. Jordan had moved into a bigger room by then so his old bedroom had a rocker and we brought that down too.

Then it was time for the bath. We both saw the large coin at the same time and looked at each other with the question of removing it, or leaving it? Well, of course it had to go. It was a coin! It was the tape that was pretty disgusting, so I gently pried it away from his skin. Not a tear, not a single one, total trust.

As I peeled away the coin, the baby's intestines started pouring out and fast! I don't know how I knew the right thing to do, but we pushed them back in and taped him up again. This was the secret: not too bad and not life threatening, double hernias. So instead of a doctor's visit, surgery. Only since I had already fed him, the procedure had to be postponed by a day. That certainly wasn't pleasant, but a happy ending all around.

We spent three weeks recovering at my father's house. Karen was great with the baby, who liked to bathe in the kitchen sink and smiled a lot. We rocked him to lullabies Dad taught me and my father sang a few. His first grandchild was home in America and now the next step was to stand before the Ark in Temple and name him. I gave him Karen's father's name Joseph, as his Hebrew name because I felt this was an honor to her and I was very emotionally connected now that I was a mom myself. James didn't make the ceremony. Maybe he didn't realize how important it was to me, but the young doctor did. And when the rabbi called for the parents to bring up the baby for the naming and blessing, he stood right next to me, and we never said a word.

Chapter Twenty-One

Now I was a new mom, far from family and learning to cope with all the media attention surrounding our little boy. Initially, it was exciting. The TV station wanted an exclusive interview and a well-known magazine wrote a story about us. We were in the newspapers because Matthew was only one of a few adoptions that actually went through and he was the youngest. Initially, I had only good intentions of helping other couples and actually volunteered at an agency to counsel other couples; but I soon realized that it might draw too much attention to us and that could prove to be dangerous. I was right.

At first, the big hurdle was to make Matthew a naturalized American citizen. Even though in Romania he was considered our child, in America he was only here on a visa and Romanian passport. I contacted our congressman and a local attorney to file the paperwork. This seemed to be taking forever, as I found out our original fingerprints were smudged and no one contacted us for new ones! So living in close proximity to Washington, D.C. I just took Matthew in my arms to the Capitol, walked the halls to find my congressman's office, plopped the baby on the secretary's desk, and said "Do you think the congressman could make a phone call on my behalf?" Totally outrageous to even think of now, but bear and cub come to mind and Matthew was adorable. No one could resist his big blue eyes and the phone call was made to INS that day. I marched in to the offices in Baltimore, again with the baby in my arms, escorted into the main office where a photo was taken and Matthew was officially sworn in. I can't imagine anything like that ever taking place now. Loads of security even to park, but a beautiful baby boy with a story opens a lot of doors. So does a determined mother.

On February 22nd, 1991, Matthew officially became a documented American citizen. We took pictures in front of the Capitol and the Washington Memorial, with the same flag he wore coming home on the plane from Romania.

Oscar with grandson Matt. (Brand Family Collection.)

I had recently rented a small space on Antique Row, where my mother-in-law helped me set up a little shop. At first I kept the baby in a small cradle behind the counter and on weekdays, Jim took care of him on weekends while I worked. But we soon realized that I needed some help. Our neighbors had a friend who was a nice elderly Japanese woman who was looking to be a nanny. She was kind, gentle and a WWII bride. She had a number of friends in our neighborhood and I felt very much at ease with her. She took care of Matthew until he was two. The separation anxiety he felt when I left for work in the morning seemed a bit over the top, but I was reassured it was natural.

I was exhausted. I loved working and coming home to my darling little man, as I called him, but because Jim was the primary wage-earner, it was I who got up at night, at least four times, to attend to Matthew. He just never seemed to adjust to the time change. He took long naps, three hours by day, then was up constantly at night. I know intellectually I could have let him cry, but I had made that promise, so I just toughed it out. Until the day I came home early, found my nanny asleep, and Matt wondering around the house alone. I gently closed the door, and noisily reentered. I never embarrassed her, but told her I was thinking of staying home and raising Matt myself. She seemed to understand and there were no hard feelings.

Which brings me to "the visit." The Romanians were coming! A surprise, yes, but also a chance to show how well we had done by them and that we were worthy. Besides, they had never seen America; and Washington, D.C. is about as American as you can get.

The entourage would include the young Dr. and his new wife as interpreters, and the amazing Dr. D and her sister. The plan was to give a grand tour of all the historic sites and make a wonderful dinner; then they would go home happy, knowing that everything turned out so well. But that's not how it went. After a tour of the White House, monuments, and beautiful little town where we lived, I took the ladies to my shop and they picked out a piece of jewelry for themselves as gifts.

I'm not sure if they understood this was vintage costume jewelry, but it seemed to make everyone so happy. I showed them the articles about the adoption in the local papers, which was a huge mistake in retrospect, but I thought they would like to know how everyone was so supportive. All they saw was money. The money we spent, borrowed, the beautiful home, filled with antiques from family and my shop, with the jewelry we could afford to give away. Such a terrible misunderstanding.

Everyone left with hugs and kisses, but soon the phone calls started; and they were threatening. They wanted money for their nephew; he deserved it and we had it. The threat seemed very real to me, although the worst they could do was tell the birthmother where we lived, but that was enough to make me nervous. I called my attorney, and he assured me that any gift I made was just that, not bribery and that threatening an American citizen in this way could lead to deportation, I just had to report it.

I decide not to answer the phone for a few days. It really was too bad. But in retrospect, a yearly visit and a reminder as Matt got older wasn't really important, there were so many other challenges ahead.

Chapter Twenty-Two

I think I have suggested that Matthew was very attached from day one to me. We never went anywhere without him. So when a vacation trip on the QE2 was in the offering because my father had been hired as the entertainer, we jumped at the chance to take Matthew and go. Dad had recorded several "Bawdy Sea Shanty" albums, and he had plenty of sea songs in his repertoire and he was scheduled for only one concert. (Kris Kristofferson was the headliner.)

The cruise had been changed to accommodate a brand new route to New Brunswick, Canada. The ship was getting old, and its usual crossing to England was getting too expensive, so this was a trial run. First stop Martha's Vineyard, then Maine and on to Canada. Exciting. And we signed on. A chance to spend time mixing my little family with Dad.

What could possibly go wrong? First of all, the performers stayed in first class, which was nice. But we could afford just above steerage. I just assumed, wrongly, that we would at least have dinner together. Bt there were very strict rules about that, and for the very first time in my life I was not invited, nor allowed to dine with my father. He was in the "Queen's Lounge" and we were in the dining room. I never felt more like Cinderella in my life, but I didn't say anything. My brother Jordan ate with the folks; though he probably would have enjoyed our company more!

At port we all took the day trips together; but back on the boat, we never saw them. Then literally on the last night heading back to New York, the ship was late leaving Martha's Vineyard, and the tide had changed. There we were eating dinner, with Matt alone with a babysitter in our room, celebrating our 10th wedding anniversary, when we heard the most ghastly noise! Years later, when the movie *Titanic* came out and it hit the iceberg, *that* was the noise – like a giant roar and shaking of this monstrous ship. I stood up and started to run. Jim shouted at me: "Where are you going?" I shouted back: "To the baby!" Later it would be reported that some woman panicked and shouted "My baby, my baby!" Yes, that was me folks.

The captain came on the loud speaker to announce we had hit the rocks off Martha's Vineyard and we were listing to one side. Everyone should remain calm; it was a two hulled ship and we were in no danger of sinking. A band would play all night for anyone who needed to relax while arrangements were being made for inspection of the hull in the morning. Oh, sure! I believe you! There's water in the hall and I'm sleeping in my life jacket!

The next morning, as promised, scuba divers assessed the damage. My father's concert of shipwreck songs was becoming a funny joke, and we had heard that the big shot film star Kris Kristofferson had a helicopter pick him up earlier that morning. About 4000 plus people just stranded. Sure, not too far out to sea and not in any real danger. But all had expected to be back in NY that afternoon.

Another announcement blared that ferry boats would come to take passengers off the boat, 250 people at a time. There was no distinction between passengers. A lottery would be held and that's how they would determine who would disembark first. Uh Huh. I looked at Jim and said pack up, we're going over to first class. My father, Karen, and brother Jordan were in the lounge when we arrived, Dad whipped out his guitar and entertained to make the time pass. When the first lottery tickets were drawn, big surprise, the first class passengers were going first. I took the baby Matt in my arms and said to Jim: "Follow my father." Down five decks and out the door to the waiting ferry. One person put his hand on my shoulder to ask for my ticket, and then dropped it. I had a baby in my arms.

Dad gave an interview on the ferry, as there was already press, with more waiting on the dock. As the big ship got smaller in our view, I was reminded of all those lullabies we heard as kids. Size doesn't matter, the sea and what lies below will triumph. When we arrived, so much press was there, my brother Jordan was being interviewed, and some lady was looking for the woman who had screamed about her child, so they interviewed me too. Little did I know that in Southampton, NY my in-laws were watching the news and saw us! I kept Matt's face hidden from the camera, and the History Channel runs that footage whenever they do a "Ship Disasters" special.

We had a nice bus ride back to NY, and were assured that we would receive our luggage in a few days. Instead of sticking around for vouchers or complaints, we took the Long Island Railroad home to my father's house to wait. Jim left to go back to Washington the next day; but it took three weeks to even be notified where we might find our luggage in a giant holding warehouse. But I was simply glad to be safe and made up funny T-shirts for the family that said: "I survived the QE2." We learned a giant hole had been ripped in the ship about the size of a football field, it was towed and overhauled, and that was my last cruise.

Life is an adventure. I thought by now that I'd had had my quota, and more than my fifteen minutes of fame.

Chapter Twenty-Three

Fame is a funny thing. Some people go in search of it; and some have it thrust upon them through no fault of their own. I find it interesting to have been on both sides. I understand what drove my father. He really started his life thinking he would have nothing to offer because of his polio. Then entertaining the troops after WWII became his introduction to a wider appreciation and then of course his radio show enabled every single artist, well known or launching a career, to have a place to showcase their talents. I was always very proud of him and again wanted to be part of his life and share this unique man with my son. What I did not want, was Thanksgiving on TV as we had done in 1970, when Bill Boggs hosted a daytime talk show. Or running to the city as a standby guest for Barry Farber with dinner after at one in the morning. I was trying for "normal" whatever that meant.

In 1996, my father was presented with the Peabody Award for excellence in broadcasting. The Folksong Festival had just turned 50 years old, already a record for a program with a single host. He was sharing this award with Oprah Winfrey. I desperately wanted to attend the ceremony. I believe his publishing house, TRO, took a large table and my husband I were invited to the Waldorf Astoria; it was a really big deal.

One tiny little problem was that at 6 years old, Matt was still extraordinarily attached to me. We had tried babysitters, with bribes: the *present gets unwrapped after mom and dad leave* sort of bribes. I was not working. I tried a preschool when he was four, but I sat outside the window reading for the three hours he was inside; finally they asked us both to leave! We got kicked out of preschool! Then I found a lovely little co-op nursery school which needed mothers to volunteer in the classroom once a week and rotate carpools. I volunteered and carpooled every day with no complaints. Finally, after a few months, the teacher said that he was ready. Matt sat under her desk but didn't cry. I was never late to pick him up and made some excellent friends there. By the time kindergarten rolled around I knew we were going to have trouble. So no guess work, I became the entertainment coordinator for his school and the first person I booked was my father!

Everyone was so excited that Oscar the Grouch was coming to their school. Big assembly and some very disappointed kids when a trash mouthed green monster didn't show up. But by the time my Dad got going with his sing-a-long and party songs, the kids loved him. I booked him every year and my brother's magic act too, so Matt was a popular kid, with mom just an office away.

This is how I got the idea to become Dad's agent down in Washington and to make sure we got regular visits. I used an old marketing trick. I would call a library or school and let them know that Oscar Brand was going to be here on such and such a date and that his lodging and travel were already covered, so this was a great opportunity for them. It worked so well, that I kept it up for about ten years. Once the World Folk Music Association became part of the process, I didn't have to do anything but sell CD's.

This was a professional organization, founded by Dick Cerri and Tom Paxton. No one got paid, but there were plenty of chances to pay tributes to legends, and make great contacts. Plus it made my father well-known again in my area and all my friends always attended the concerts. Full house every single time. I'm not trying to take credit for his re-establishing his performing career. It's just that I'm not sure the internet played a big part in a '60s folk fan's life. Most people did not know that he was still on the air and could be live streamed on Saturday nights.

Now when the invitation to sit at the table for the Peabody Award presented itself, I was all excited. The little family drove to New York and Matt stayed with my old friend Dana from the Village days. We had reconnected over our mutual need to adopt and Matt had a good friend in her daughter and trusted the situation, since we visited every summer and vacationed with my Dad in New York.

Every single person alive in Broadcasting was there that afternoon. I sat with my husband to my left and Karen to my right; the other people were clients of hers and people from TRO. When I went to check my coat, no one was at the counter, so Peter Jennings took my coat, jumped over the counter and hung it up for me. Nice man. Found out later, when I told Dad about this funny incident, that my father had dated Peter Jennings wife before he did, and they'd had a gentleman's distaste for each other after that. Good thing I didn't have to put my name on the claim check.

Next stop the ladies room; everyone had to go. I was on line with Oprah, who remarked that she liked my dress, and I responded that I wouldn't eat hamburgers because of her, to which she responded: "Get over it, I have!"

Explains a lot, I guess. Then on the way back to the table I spotted Barbara Walters. Never one to be star-struck, I only approached her to tell her about adopting one of the Romanian children she had done a story about. But I could tell immediately by her body language that she was in deep conversation with a gentlemen. She turned and introduced the President of CBS! Then politely asked how my son was doing and I just said "thriving." Clearly this was some kind of negotiation that I had the misfortune of interrupting, but I wasn't worried about Ms. Walters, she could take care of herself, so I shook the ice off my shoulders and went inside to the ceremony.

Tom Brokaw introduced the award, with great fanfare: the audio recording of the Weavers choosing their name live on the air of Dad's show, and a video of some of the artists. You can see this by looking it up on YouTube. Mr. Brokaw was eloquent and full of praise as he introduced Dad. I welled up with tears as my father took the podium, and reached for Karen's hand, thinking we were sharing the same pride and emotions, but she quickly withdrew it. I never tried anything like that again. The rebuff was obviously because she had clients there, I am sure she must have been emotional too. But it wasn't going to be a moment for us, that was clear, and we never had another like it.

Too bad. I learned my lesson again. But it was a wonderful night and I felt those familiar pulls of New York in my heart again. There had been a special fiftieth broadcast party, at Cooper Union Great Hall. I just felt I was missing out, but back to my life in Washington, with a promise to travel if anything else dramatic turned up. Oh, good; it didn't take long.

My brother Jordan was graduating from Exeter Academy, on his way to Harvard the following fall. He loved the crew team and the whole family went to watch him row at the famous "Head of the Charles" race. Matt and I took the elevator down first as Jim was tying his shoes in the hall and I didn't want to miss the race. By the time we got to the shoreline, the race had already begun, so Matt and I ran alongside the river until we got to the end. It was such a close finish that someone shouted from the other side: *Did you see who won?* Of course, I called it for Exeter, I saw my brother's boat first, and I did! We were so excited and hitched a ride back to the boathouse, where my father was waiting with Jim. He was furious with me, he said, you must never do that again, always wait, and don't leave your husband behind. I would have missed the whole race, but that wasn't his point, still teaching from his mistakes, and I was burning, thinking of the Lincoln Tunnel and being stranded. Okay, point made. How embarrassing and deflating on a glorious afternoon.

Next there were the festivities. My brother had taken classical guitar lessons, but was in a punk rock band playing in the square. So we walked around a little and absorbed the atmosphere. Very different high school experience for him, wonderful campus and boarding school, with parents who visited on weekends and took an interest in everything. No jealousy here. I learned later, that this was more of a microscope than living at home. But at that time we weren't close enough to share those tidbits. He was a teenager, off to College, and his older sister was a mother. Siblings yes, but with an entirely different perspective. Of course, so much revealed later about his struggle for freedom, makes me wish I had reached out a little more.

In the summer of 1997, we were spending the July 4th holiday with my folks on Long Island. So many years had passed since the accident, so I overcame fear again and went. Every year, they were invited to a special party on the beachfront property of one of Karen's clients. That year, my brother Jordan had broken his foot, so he planted himself in a beach chair while the party surrounded him. A shuttle cart took us down from the big house to the beach. It was a great adventure for Matt, at seven, but really hard on my father who was limping badly, and having trouble with his hip. I was looking out for him because at 77 he seemed fragile to me. Later, when he had hip surgery, he told me he wished he hadn't waited so long; he felt great again, and continued performing well into his late 80's.

At this party, were any number of eligible girls for my teenage brother to meet according to my stepmother. However, the most stunningly brilliant and gorgeous, blue-eyed girl sat beside him the entire night. The kind of immediate attraction you may notice, but have to look away. These two people never stopped talking. Her name was Torrie and her father had just discovered the wreck of Blackbeard's ship, *The Queen Anne's Revenge*. Her father was all over the news and had been invited to the party by dint of his new found fame; he brought his daughter, now my sister-in-law.

From the moment they met, they were inseparable. This young woman was a force of nature. She moved with my brother to Boston, spent his entire Harvard undergraduate life with him and then Harvard Medical School. Her influence led him to become a vegan and a generous father, and helped him develop the ability to juggle all the responsibilities of being an intern and then a resident in a busy NY hospital. Later, the young couple moved to California to pursue a more idyllic life.

We are very close, we have the brothers/sister visit once a year. But I have to commend Torrie for sticking around under great pressure. They met in 1997, but didn't marry until 2003: a gorgeous, full blown wedding extravaganza on the water in Sag Harbor. Her last and final gift, from her father who passed away soon after. I will never forget how he sought me out the morning after the wedding. He could tell how much I loved my brother. He said: "Please take care of my girl." We have been great friends ever since. She is a challenging personality and never boring, which is why I think we get along. She has overcome great barriers to get what she wants – raising two brilliant, wonderful children, who are loving, kind and generous. Most of all, Torrie recognized very early the inequities of our status in the family. She has fought hard to make sure that I am included in all family gatherings.

My favorite story takes place after Jordan's graduation from medical school. The very next day we were all staying in Stockbridge, MA. Dad had a booking at the Guthrie Center, which was the original church in the story of Arlo Guthrie's *Alice's Restaurant*. Jordan and John Foley were his back up players and there was a little kitchen with a premade dinner served first. That evening the waitress didn't show up. There were only two for a sold out performance. I said I would volunteer to serve. I'd never done it before, but I made an announcement that I was Oscar's daughter and just pitching in, and that all tips would go to the Guthrie Center. My stepmother suggested that it was somehow unseemly for me to do this. But I did it anyway, figuring a happy crowd was better than an unhappy, hungry one. (I also gained so much respect for how difficult a job it is. I mean, if you want sugar with your coffee, tell me before I go to the kitchen and back!) We made money for the Center, and the show was a great success. At the same time, I got a taste of what was to become the next fifteen years of helping to arrange and manage shows for Dad.

That same summer was the discovery of what was to become one of my favorite vacations of all time. My father was performing at a National Landmark Preserve called The Mohonk Mountain House.

Waiting tables at the Guthrie Center with sister-in-law Torrie.
(Brand Family Collection.)

125 years old at the time, Mohonk had originally served as a getaway for the very rich and famous from the big city. It is unique because the drive to the top of the mountain is two miles on a thin dirt road, no fences on the side. Many losses they never talk about, but we were there one year when a car went over in a fog. Upon arrival at the Mountain House, your car is taken away. Now some people stay a week, some the whole summer, but a car is never needed. The Lake House sits on a naturally formed glacial body of water, stocked every season with trout for fishing, a log for balancing, a beach for swimming and many paths for hiking. There

are no television sets in the rooms and the décor is antique with an actual parlor for playing board games. All the food is local and tea is served on the porch at 4 PM daily. It's a real family resort.

This is where my father invited us for the two days he was entertaining in the great room. We had no idea, that first visit, that this was such a spectacular place. By the time we arrived, as the Giant Stone Castle revealed itself, we were hooked. The gardens were spectacular, with a maze of trees just for fun. We took a carriage ride to the top of the mountain where you could see five states from the lookout. I could never begin to describe the beauty of this place, with the old barn, horses, manicured lawns for croquet matches. This was heaven for everyone. The place you see and never forget, the place that takes you back in time as if you lived it.

I had no idea when we arrived that this was an all-inclusive, expensive place. We were guests of the entertainer. Mohonk has two important distinction. One, is that it is a family resort, so the entertainment is always old-fashioned square-dancing, folk music, or a lecture series about nature. The other is that there is no air-conditioning, in keeping with the absolute tradition of antiquity. (This would later change, as the resort updated in 2012 to include a spa and compete for travel dollars).

The Smiley family had run Mohonk for five generations and one of the daughters had married a nice man who was a huge fan of folk music. Getting Oscar Brand to sing and stay at his resort was a real coup. So a family coming along was no big deal. We had assigned seating, and unlike the QE2 fiasco, we all sat together. My father received people throughout the meal and, as always, being gracious and approachable.

Jordan and my folks had what they call the Tower Room: a cylinder shaped huge suite with a gorgeous lakeside view. We had a small room with a valance overlooking the mountain, which turned out to be nice, because as anyone who has had experience with lakes will know: sound travels.

The concert was wonderful, although I believe with all the

people stuffed into the room, the temperature may have reached over 100 degrees, even at night. Afterwards, we retired to our rooms, where immediately upon laying down, the smoke alarms started going off because of the heat. I was beside myself, since I'm so sensitive to sound. Jim tried to disarm it while I went to the front desk, a good walk away, where I was told that the main switch was down the mountain and the noise couldn't be turned off. We slept on and off all night and in the morning at breakfast we asked if this had bothered my father. He said they didn't hear it! I am thinking they were on a different circuit and I started to feel badly about how I had behaved since I was a guest. Dad did one more children's concert in the morning and then Matt and his Dad went for a hike.

By the time we met up for a cookout on the hilltop, it was apparent that the path they took was for serious climbers only. I was upset, but kept it to myself, since they had lived to tell the tale. This was the trip that cemented my son's lifelong passion for fishing. All he had was a little line and hook, but as soon as he felt that first bite, that was it.

We were going to visit more often. Not just Mohonk because we loved it, but my father's place, because by that summer they had decided to buy a boat. Actually, Karen bought the boat for Jordan to have fun with his friends. It was a motorboat moored in Manhasset Bay. The thing was that my father adored sailing. But his little sunfish, was not adequate for taking seriously. The sunfish was dispatched to Jean Ritchie's house on the hill, to sit and gather moss and the motorboat, which they named "Tsunami," became the weekend outing. Or that was the intention, because as everyone knows, an inboard motor cannot be fixed unless it is taken in for repair. The worse that happens when you're sailing is that the wind dies down and you either paddle or have a little outboard to bring you home. This boat never worked when needed to entertain; it became a source of dissention and a money pit.

Now I will reveal a family secret. In the year 2000, while

vacationing at my father's home, he invited Matt and I to go out for a little spin on "the boat." Matt was hugely excited. By ten years old, he had become very attached to my father. My husband had taken a job in California, during the tech boom, so we were spending the summer with family.

I was always wary of the water. Gorgeous to look at, but not fun to be on. But it was Dad and Matt, so what could go wrong? I'm not sure if I have mentioned it before, but my father always kept a leather pouch on his belt loop. This pouch contained "the book," every single phone number and address of everyone my father ever met. Updated every year, it was golden. You can see it in many photos of him. So remember it as I tell you this story. We were just puttering around the bay, my son's little head sticking up through the pop-up window in the bow and dad standing at the wheel. I was sitting in back enjoying the nice slow speed.

One of Jean's boys, Jon, had bought a sailboat with a friend. It was moored close to shore for a little luncheon, so dad decided to get really close to say *hi*. You know, buzz the boat? At the exact moment he turned to wave, his belt loop got stuck on the throttle and he fell backwards into the boat as it went full speed directly towards the dock! No time to think or warn Matt or scream. It was one of those moments: You're either going to live or die, but your kid's head wasn't going to make it.

I'm upset just writing about it. Well, the boat hit the dock. But miraculously, instead of crashing, it lifted right out of the water as Dad killed the engine, and just as gently as that floated backward and came to a complete stop. Everyone fine. Cheers rang out from the shoreline. Dad and I looked at each other and decided then and there NEVER to tell Karen. We never did. Even Jon, who saw the whole thing, never mentioned it, and I never set foot on that boat again.

The end of "Tsunami" isn't pretty either. Some kids had a party and trashed it while in dry-dock. No one wanted to pay for restoring it, so they slapped on a "for sale" sign. It's probably still sitting in the boatyard today. Shame, once my husband expressed interest in fixing it up, but we never had the money, and he never knew the story. True sailors might say it was cursed, but I think, since we survived, it was just another bad choice. A ride on a fiberglass sunfish would have been nice.

July 2000. Jeannie and Matt at the dock, Port Washington, NY.
(Brand Family Collection.)

Except for that incident, the summer of 2000 was our best time ever. I sat on the dock all day with Matt as he fished, and we became acquainted with the "old salties," fisherman that hung around the dock. They were chivalrous and helpful to Matt, as he learned the craft, and even took him out once on a fishing expedition, after being thoroughly vetted by mom. Matt caught a giant Bluefish on that adventure and two Tunas which he gave away to hungry people who wait on the docks for food. But the three foot Bluefish, we snuck into grandma's house and put in the bathtub until morning so it could be professionally filleted.

Matt cooked it himself and I took photos to frame. I thought this was a huge moment for him, but as it turns out, bless his heart, catching and releasing little snappers is a lot easier than watching something so large struggle and die. His fishing days were over after that night.

As mentioned before, the opportunity for Jim to take a job in California was too tempting to turn down. But being a realist, I thought Matt needed stability to finish his schooling and keep our house intact. Then the tech bubble burst, along with the job market. Jim took this job loss hard. I had been so supportive of a year's trial run in California, but when his car was picked up for transport, I sat on our curb and cried. Something seemed askew. I had felt that shift again. Security was the little Cape Cod house behind me and my friends and family. I was so glad to have him back.

During the California trial, Jim visited every five weeks. During the intervals I was busy with Matt's school. Also, a friend's husband was gravely ill, so I took over helping to schedule food and visits for her boys. The night he passed away, her son stayed with us. He said it was too sad at his house. Unfortunately, I lost this friend too in an accident years later. Some people fall and get up, which happened to me; some do not. During the period of Jim's absence, Matt and I got into a lovely routine of dinner and watching *Antiques Roadshow* in bed. We were very close.

When Jim would call me from an exciting side trip to Yosemite, from the top of a mountain, wishing I was there to share the sunset, I just couldn't relate. I was angry after all the responsibility of being a single mom, and shoveling snow in February myself, doing homework, etc. I just didn't understand how much fun he was having.

When the hammer struck, and he was out of work, I thought that he would be happy to return home and use his remarkable year as bait for a great job. Sure, we had lost a lot of money. The company made you invest ten percent of your salary in their stock, which was at 60 when he signed and 18 when he left, but he was home. Yet he was so very unhappy. He spent three weeks gardening in our backyard, but I wanted him to get back on that horse and look for a job. He was angry at the world in general and me in particular, because I never visited him, although it was on the calendar to do so at the next school break.

A wonderful show was being held at the 92nd street Y. My father, Christine Lavin and other guests were performing and we went up to New York to join in. My brother Jordan was home on break and would be accompanying Dad on bass, and my brother Eric was going with his oldest son, Ezra, who was Matt's age. So this was going to be a fun family affair, and a good way for Jim to reconnect. (Even with his own family, who didn't get the move to California either and had given me the "wanderlust" verdict.)

Well, my brother and I sat together so the cousins could talk. As Christine Lavin did her famous "Sensitive New Age Guy" shtick, she had my brother Jordan and my father join in. Then she walked up the aisle looking for volunteers from the audience to come up on stage. Later she said she always looked for someone who smiled back at her, because she knew they would co-operate with her antics. Well, Eric and I had been laughing and she picked him out of an extremely crowded audience. He went onstage and finished the song.

Immediately, my father took the microphone and said: "I don't know how this happened, but you have two out of three of my sons onstage right now." Unplanned and a story forever. At the party later, Jim was introduced to Christine. We had a big laugh over it and I think he realized that he could take me to Washington, D.C. but that was about as far as I was going to go.

I needed this connection to my family, and he instinctively knew I was never going to feel secure without it. Resentment was bubbling under the surface, and we never really got over the "separation" that wasn't.

After a reasonable time, Matt was starting middle school, Jim found work and my little store was thriving. I had a friend who had a decorating shop close by, and offered housewife hours for me to come in and sometimes do a little show. I thought we were pretty stable. Stability is only an illusion for everyone. I know this. I read philosophy and live in the moment, most of the time. I had a backyard garden, house, son, job I loved, friends, husband.

We had survived the DC Sniper – the "Beltway Killer" – the year before, when our little town was under siege from an unknown gunman and school was on lockdown and you filled your gas tank while in constant motion, since this seemed to be the mad man's preferred random target. Everyone breathed a sigh of relief when he was caught with his accomplice. They had been only one block from our house, during two of the shootings. Security is an illusion, Jeannie. When will you learn?

Jeannie and Jim photobombing Oscar during the soundcheck for a D.C. Concert, 2001. (Brand Family Collection.)

Chapter Twenty-Four

Matt started his new school on September 8th thereabouts, 2001. Nice new building, some old friends from his old school and a bus to take him there. So I was free, no complaints. September 11th, 2001: where were you? Everyone remembers. I was getting my hair done, when the news said that the World Trade Center was on fire. Being a New Yorker and a child of the sixties, I didn't need to hear more. By the time the second Tower was hit I was already calling Jim to pick up Matt at school; this was the apocalypse that was simmering deep in my subconscious my whole life.

Of course I ran for the usual: duct tape, plastic window dressing, canned items, dog food, water, all the time listening to the news on the radio. I figured at least 3 weeks in the basement before the dust settled. The mattresses flew down the stairs as I got home and heard about the Pentagon. OK, they're here. Next, Jim and Matt came in and Matt was ashen, they hadn't even made an announcement yet at his school and when he was called out of class and saw his Dad there to pick him up, he thought I was dead. Mom was always the one in an emergency. We explained what was happening, and we were just being cautious. One hour later, everyone was sent home. So I wasn't wrong, just a little quicker on the draw.

I don't need to tell a big story here. Everyone knew someone, or more than one. Life changed again forever. There is nothing that feels stable, and *control* is an illusion, but our family in New York survived and so did we. A sniper and then 9/11. Well you have to think maybe Matt had some issues beyond our scaring him, and you would be right. Those scars are deep and you just never know how they will manifest, until they do.

We had an inkling of trouble on the return from Massachusetts, after the Guthrie Center show. We had left Matt with his favorite

Uncle John. He had been having a glass of wine on the porch one night when Matt asked if he could spend the night with a friend. The question was is this OK with your parents? The answer was *yes*, so off he went, to climb to the top of the abandoned old schoolhouse, probably to get high, who knows. But when a noise was heard, the boys jumped and Matt injured his leg. The first of many unexplained injuries, but he didn't go home. The teenagers followed a pretty classmate to her house and egged it when she wouldn't come out. Matt being the only recognized kid, was caught as the boys ran away. I was notified immediately upon returning what had happened.

This wasn't the first time punishment was in order. I had had my trials as has any parent, but it's a choice how to punish and I followed my father's lead. James, coming from a strict upbringing was constantly afraid and never took the blame for even the smallest infraction, like spilling something. It was always someone else's fault because he had strict punishment imbedded in his brain and was hard wired for hurt.

So I went the way of Mark Twain. When Matt as a young child swore out loud at a playdate, he was instructed to buy paint at the local hardware store with his own money and paint over all the graffiti in our town park. So on the occasion of egging a friend's house, a bottle of Windex and a hose, and he spent the day cleaning. So far I had only heard the words "I hate you" once. It was at my brother's wedding when I wouldn't buy him a pack of cigarettes. I had no idea that cigarettes were the least of his problems.

By 2006, my father turned 86 and he appeared for the last time at a concert near our town. Still drawing a sold out crowd, he introduced one song but then sang another. No one paid attention, but I caught it. He seemed a little frailer and he sang the same song in the second set that he had in the first. So we decided this was the last time he would travel so far for a gig. We'd visit more often. I would represent him at tribute concerts and that worked out. Either his face projected on a big screen, while I made a little speech, or maybe a recording. It worked. So the biggest surprise to me was when at my 50 birthday party, with all friends and business associates invited, my folks showed up, as a surprise. It was the first and only time I can remember them doing anything as a couple strictly for me.

My magician brother James came up from Georgia, where he was now living, and put on a grand illusion show. Then he introduced my father as "Mr. Show Business" and Dad gave a speech about me, which was endearing, unforgettable, and I had to look up half the words he used later. My perfect memory, my beautiful night, everyone still alive and healthy. My little speech as I cut the cake was just to say that everyone I loved was in that room. Although, secretly I was scanning it for my son, who had disappeared earlier with his friend to sneak upstairs to a sweet sixteen party. Okay, teenagers, it stings, but no harm done. Or so I thought, but the only photo I have of him at that party shows him heavy-lidded and obviously stoned.

By sixteen years old, we had an obvious problem. Matt wanted to learn to drive, and frankly I was so tired of getting up early for those ridiculous high school hours that I agreed. My husband wanted him to have a big, safe car, so we took our tax refund to Carmax and set him up with a large Maxima. We called him from the salesroom and woke him from a deep sleep to tell him he had a car. Boy, we were so naïve. I would be bouncing off the walls if my parents bought me a car. He went back to sleep.

By the time he was in eleventh grade and dating an older girl, a senior, we had already had a few misdemeanor charges of possession which required either a class or community service.

We paid fines, got up at 2 AM to bail him out of jail, gave grounding punishments, and didn't think that it was any more serious than teenage angst. Besides, I saw a lot worse, and I never experienced this sort of behavior myself, so I had no way of gauging if this was a serious problem. Matt was always sorry and knowing my background, extremely sensitive to all my emotional confusion over whether this was just bad luck at getting caught over what everyone does, or a problem.

By the time my son was in his senior year, no one, including Matt thought he would graduate. Finally, a brilliant senior project and a private plea to the guidance counselor insured the Friday before graduation that he had enough credits. Even at Constitution Hall that next Monday, when he walked across the stage and they handed him his diploma, Matt was convinced it was for show. He didn't realize that the envelope is always empty in case the line-up is shuffled around.

Matt's graduation, 2008. (Brand Family Collection.)

Then one night, at a party, someone made a move on his girl. Matt stood up to block a punch, and he took a hit to his jaw. Broken, badly, he came home, angry and yelling. I looked at the way his jaw was hanging and his teeth were moving and we rushed him to the hospital. He was examined in front of me, gave permission to the doctors, and started to rattle off the drugs in his system. I wasn't surprised. By that time, I was just devastated.

He needed very risky surgery which had a 25% chance of paralyzing his face, or go with the less risky repair, which meant 24 hour care and his jaw being wired shut for 6 weeks. By the time the painkillers started wearing off, sixteen hours into this drama, he was taken into surgery. What we didn't know at that time was to ask if insurance covered it. One hour later, it would have been another doctor and the answer would be yes, but at the time, you don't think, you act. There goes the college fund, right into his mouth, along with everything I thought I knew about my son.

Always the caregiver, and exhausted, at some horrifying hour of the morning, the hospital decided to dismiss him into my care. The nurse gave me a long tube to insert down his throat, in case he choked in the middle of the night, and a scissors. They wanted to send him home because there was no one in recovery that night. I'm positive of this, but I needed a little recovery too. It was not to be. I stayed up all night by his bedside, in case he stopped breathing or vomited and I would have to save his life, again.

Even though we had a whole summer to recover, and my father sent the "bottomless pit of love" advice along with a signed copy of his *Bawdy Songbook*, I knew this was the beginning of something bigger and more ominous. I made ice cream shakes and timed his medicine, crushing it into a sweet tea or a protein drink. He was ornery and angry.

I understood because this was no way to spend the summer, but I also had no idea that he was going through a partial withdrawal. How would I know? The friends stopped by in the beginning, the girl broke up with him, but still visited, all this going on a summer before senior year. I felt terrible for him, and by July 4th weekend we had both had enough of each other. The dental surgeon checked him out and said he was doing fine. Two more weeks, and Matt was begging to go out with friends, so I said *yes*.

His first time out in weeks, no worries, and his jaw was wired shut. He was 125 pounds of contrition. What could he possibly do that would be any worse than what he had survived? Plus, we had to show him that we trusted him and that we believed he'd learned his lesson, physically and mentally.

The story, as I believe to be true to this day, goes something like this. Matt visited old friends and had two beers, on an empty stomach with a jaw wired, maybe not a great idea. He went to sulk in the woods near his old hangout with his girlfriend and then headed home. He had borrowed my car. Immediately he felt a pull to the right and knew he had a flat. So he did the prudent thing: find a place to pull into and change the tire. Unfortunately for him and the family and life in general, he pulled into a cul-de-sac and driveway of a police officer and his police officer wife. They were upset, the motor was running, but Matt was stopping to call and let us know what happened. At that exact moment, and without warning, a man pulled him from the car, and slammed him into the concrete driveway, cracking his jaw again.

Matt told me later, that he felt at least nothing could feel worse than this, but he was wrong, because the man picked him up and dragged him to the sidewalk where he slammed him into the ground again. Then he left Matt laying there and called for a back-up on-duty officer to get the kid in his driveway to the hospital.

By the time we heard anything, it was from Matt, who had lost consciousness and regained it in the ambulance. The officer was very nice and dropped him off at the nearest hospital, along with all his possessions, which was strange and no sobriety tests because of the jaw being wired, just a blood test Matt had consented to give. Jim and I raced to the hospital to find Matt in the parking lot, we took him back to the original hospital to check his jaw, and sure enough it was broken again and in other places.

Nurses and doctors coming and going, but I never left his side.

I was convinced we had a problem now, and requested an evaluation, hoping someone could help us figure out how to help this distraught young man. I didn't know any of the story yet, but when a male nurse tried to remove me from the room while they did some tests, Matt became very agitated. The man said he would call security if I refused to leave, which I did, all 102lbs of me! By the time Jim arrived with crackers and tea for breakfast, the scene was just chaotic and bizarre.

After examination by a social worker the news came back that Matt loved his family, felt very protected and secure with us and just wanted to go home. I should have felt relieved. I didn't. I was hoping she would say that he needed help and they would keep him for a while and straighten out all his problems for me, returning him to us whole and happy. That was my secret wish, but I acted relieved and loving, as I am trained to do, and brought my son home.

Promises were made, his friends talked him into a lawsuit against the police for the beating he took without provocation or warning. I secretly hid all the knives and sharp objects in our house and went with him for his first consult with a lawyer to show support. We found someone right away who saw the injustice of what happened, but filed too soon, so that suddenly four citations, four months later, were filed against Matt for his conduct and his alcohol blood test. The video for the parking lot never surfaced, and although we showed our support for all he had been through, his anger just built and built. He had no painkillers for the extra broken jaw after two weeks. I'm guessing that's when he started self-medicating. By the time he went to court and was thrown in jail, a complete surprise to everyone and certainly the lawyer defending him, he was ruined. Whether they humiliated him or not, I never knew, but he changed completely.

He needed anxiety medication, which I'm sure he mixed with

alcohol. He had night sweats and nightmares. He didn't believe in justice at all.

When my mother-in-law passed away, he got his first tattoo, her name across his chest, but was too drunk to attend the funeral, arriving late and crushing our hopes that the family would somehow be strong enough to put him back together. More tattoos followed. He dropped out of community college, where he had been given a scholarship for the automotive repair division. He was and is extremely talented with cars, but didn't have the patience for sitting in class. He wanted to work.

Thinking this was his best opportunity to have discipline, I agreed when he got a job at the local country club, not realizing yet again, that the culture of a club is all about drinking. I am writing about this chapter in our lives because it's not only a cautionary tale, but also because I can see how even the best of intentions and need to keep private family matters private can lead to devastating results.

In 2011, my son overdosed on a combination of drugs and alcohol. Again, he was lucky enough to have someone drag him into the street, so they wouldn't be associated with the 911 call they were about make. He walked into the house like nothing had happened, and we had no idea. Until this "friend" knocked on our door and told us.

Everyone will tell you that a person has to want to change. No forced rehabilitation will do it – as we can easily see from the countless celebrity stories that wind up in relapse or death. Matt decided on his own that he had had enough of this life. Good for him, he chose his own path for recovery and has been diligent and clean ever since, with a full-time job and a morning meeting ever since for four years. Happy ending, sure, if you believe in them. The court settled a very small amount for only medical expenses, which after lawyers and fees, was pretty much what we like to call a "moral" victory.

He met a nice women with children. I'm thrilled about this,

because to tell you the truth, grandchildren are for my friends. I'm just tired of all of it. I love kids, especially other people's, and for a short amount of time. Maybe, after all is written and read, it's apparent that I was put on this earth to care for as many broken, rejected, and damaged people as I did. As Dad would say: "I hope it all works out for you." And he meant it.

Oscar singing at a World Folk Music Association Showcase, 2005.
(Photo courtesy Chuck Morse.)

Epilogue

I wanted my son to grow up knowing my father. Mission accomplished. The entire family and the dog, listens to the Folksong Festival on Saturday nights, streaming it live on the Internet. I am still amazed how many people text or write to me about something my father did along the way that helped their careers. I find photos on the Internet of him in places I never knew he went. Or I hear a radio broadcast of an interview with Harry Belafonte or Yves Montand. As an adult I know how involved he was with the folk movement; as a child, I just liked having him around because he was funny and warm and always singing.

The one thing I hope I have expressed is that I believe this multi-talented man was more than just a musician. I have seen hundreds of concerts and even though the playlist might vary little, I was never ever bored, always entertained, and amazed at his longevity in this business. At one time he even wrote a play for Agnes de Mille, who also wrote the Foreword to his book *The Ballad Mongers*. So many different avenues of this very fickle business; maybe that's why he lasted as long as he has.

As I write this, I am sorry to say that our beloved Jean passed away last year. Her tribute concert was the most memorable, emotional, night I have experienced in my lifetime. Everyone gathered together to sing and share stories. Jon calling me his "God-sister," as he introduced me to the packed church. It threw me. I was only expecting "Oscar Brand's daughter," but he understood how powerful the connection was. I read a prepared statement from Dad. Then the church filled with the trilling voice of Jean Ritchie and Oscar Brand, singing a song from one of their live recordings. They were laughing and teasing each other. The speakers were set on the ceiling so the sound seemed to come from above. In a church, this is especially touching and moving and everyone was crying. I ran to the back to compose myself, and everyone crowded around me, sending love and good wishes back to my father. That would have been wonderful to do, but instead I hopped a cab to my hotel and returned home to Washington the next day. That was November of last year, by then my father was not receiving company.

Dad was still producing his show at the age of 96, with the help of Jean's son Jon, who lived with my family for three years after George passed and Jean went to live in Kentucky. Last summer, there was an opening of an exhibit at the, Museum of the City of New York, about the Folk Era. I didn't go, but my father made his last public appearance there and saw his old friend Fred Hellerman. I can tune in to YouTube if I want to see them sing "This Land is Your Land" that night.

My brothers and I are all very close, and we get together once a year, always joking that this will be the last time we can pull this off, but we're luckier than most, and have always managed.

A few years ago, my brother Jordan and his young family were visiting *Clearwater's Great Hudson River Revival*, started so long ago by Pete Seeger and friends. Just by coincidence, my brother's youngest son Atticus came up to Pete with his curly haired, mischievous grin. Pete tousled his hair, remarking on the curls, having no idea that this was his old pal's grandson. My brother never said a word. That's just life, full of amazing people and stories to tell.

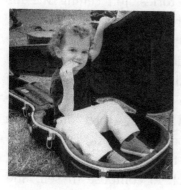

Atticus Brand, Oscar's youngest grandchild, at Clearwater's Great Hudson River Revival, Croton, NewYork, 2011. (Photo by Torrie Lloyd-Masters Brand.)

And now I'm writing this final note on Saturday night, November 19, 2016. I wish with all my heart that I was tuning in with my family for an archive program at 10 PM, "Under the light of yon municipal moon." Then I would be calling my dad with my "review".

But on September 30th, at the age of 96, he went to join the big "Hootenanny" in the sky. The outpouring of love and stories, seem never ending and overwhelming. I held a memorial of my own, near my home in Maryland. I read his lyrics and an excerpt from this book. Many tributes are planned for the future and the newspapers were full of wonderful stories, mostly confirming what I already knew. Dad had such amazing talent and was beloved by so many, so mostly stories of how he had helped them on their way up.

Oscar and his kids. From left: James, Oscar, Jeannie, Eric, and Jordan holding his newborn daughter. (Photo by Torrie Lloyd-Masters Brand.)

Yet almost every obituary had the same quote: "Survived by his wife of 46 years and their son, and three children from a previous marriage." That last part is why I wrote this book. I am not a footnote. I am his daughter and his legacy. On my last visit, I whispered in his ear: "Dad, I wrote a book." He smiled. I know he always wanted me to write. I kissed his forehead and left for Maryland. Although I visited frequently this past year, there was something about that encounter that made me feel it would be my last.

So while the radio is silent tonight, his fans and his family will always remember the big voice, the jokes, the songs and the good times filled with friends and music. Three quarters of a page in the *Washington Post*, with a photo of Eleanor Roosevelt and Dad. He would have liked that.

Oscar in performance. (Photo by George Pickow.)

Acknowledgments

My husband Jim, son Matt, and three wonderful brothers for allowing me to embark upon this journey and tell the truth as I remember it. My family and friends for their support, especially Lawrence Gerzog, who reminded me of my roots and encouraged me to write about them.

The new friends I have made through social media, who have been so inspiring with wonderful stories and memories of my father.

The goodwill of all the photographers, including Torie Lloyd-Masters Brand and Steve Somerstein. And especially to Jon and Peter Pickow for allowing us to use the photographs by their father, George Pickow. And to Jac Holzman for use of album covers.

Frank Beacham for always giving my father credit in his frequent writings, and Chuck Morse of the World Folk Music Association for his gentle guidance and great respect in honoring my father. Also Dick Cerri (RIP) and the entire folk music community for reaching out and becoming my forever family. And of course my beloved godmother Jean Ritchie.

Paul Gutman for generous help.

And a special thank-you to New Street Communications, who made this project a reality.